Teach Them to
WORK

Teach Them to
WORK

*Building a Positive Work Ethic
in Our Children*

Mary Beeke

REFORMATION HERITAGE BOOKS
Grand Rapids, Michigan

Teach Them to Work
© 2021 by Mary Beeke

Reformation Heritage Books
3070 29th St. SE
Grand Rapids, MI 49512
616-977-0889
orders@heritagebooks.org
www.heritagebooks.org

Printed in the United States of America
22 23 24 25 26 27/10 9 8 7 6 5 4 3

Library of Congress Cataloging-in-Publication Data

Names: Beeke, Mary, author.
Title: Teach them to work : building a positive work ethic in our children / Mary
    Beeke.
Description: Grand Rapids, Michigan : Reformation Heritage Books, [2021] |
    Includes bibliographical references.
Identifiers: LCCN 2021001906 (print) | LCCN 2021001907 (ebook) | ISBN
    9781601788764 (paperback) | ISBN 9781601788771 (epub)
Subjects: LCSH: Parenting—Religious aspects—Christianity. | Child rearing—
    Religious aspects—Christianity. | Protestant work ethic. | Work—Religious
    aspects—Christianity. | Diligence. | Perseverance (Ethics)
Classification: LCC BV4529 .B45 2021 (print) | LCC BV4529 (ebook) | DDC
    241/.64—dc23
LC record available at https://lccn.loc.gov/2021001906
LC ebook record available at https://lccn.loc.gov/2021001907

For additional Reformed literature, request a free book list from Reformation Heritage Books at the above regular or email address.

To my dear husband Joel,
who is a worker par excellence.

Thank you for your untiring work in God's kingdom.
Thank you for your unending love,
kindness, and patience.

You are a true example of Jesus Christ
to me and others.

Contents

Preface

The short version of this book would be four words, *just do your work*:

- *Just*—Don't hesitate; just get started.
- *Do*—Do what you are called to do to the best of your ability.
- *Your*—Your work is assigned to *you*, not someone else.
- *Work*—Accomplish something useful; get the task done.

That's what diligent people do. They might even wonder why a book like this needs to be written. What's the big deal? Just do your work!

Well, this book is not for them. They don't need it. This book is for those of us who might not be naturally inclined to diligence or who have children cut from this mold. This book is for parents striving to instill a positive work ethic into the fiber of their children's personalities. This book is for parents whose children act like they are stricken with a heart attack when they have to do some work around the house. It's for parents whose children have manipulated them to do the work themselves because it's easier than the battle. This book is for parents who are left frustrated, exhausted, and defeated by the struggle.

I am qualified to write this book because I was that kid who gave my parents a hard time. I couldn't get away with showing defiance—my dad wouldn't tolerate a whisper of that—but defiance and resistance lived in my heart. My sweet mom doesn't remember the time she cried when I was trying to wriggle out of work yet again. "Mary," she said in exasperation, "you make it so hard for me." But I remember it now with tears of regret in my eyes.

I am qualified because I know all the tricks to getting out of work or, at least, putting it off. I know the mental gymnastics a lazy kid employs to find ways of avoiding the pain of labor. I know what it is to work hard to get out of work and, in the end, having to do the work anyway. I remember gradually learning to work because my parents didn't give up. I realized that if I were to respect myself and expect others to respect me, I had to *earn* that respect by working hard. I finally learned the joys and the rewards of accomplishment and the satisfaction of a job well done.

Since that time, I have been a student, a nurse, a teacher, a wife, a mother, and now a grandmother. I've had the opportunity to observe and work with many children and adults. The variety of personalities I've seen has been fascinating, and I have learned so much from them. It has been interesting to see their behavior, hear their words, and try to figure out what makes them tick. Of all the subjects I have ever studied, I find human nature the most intriguing.

Yet, despite all these experiences, I feel unqualified to write this book because I have shortcomings and have made plenty of mistakes (though I trust I have learned lessons through them). I know many others much more qualified to pontificate on this subject of work than I am, so I've interviewed some of these "expert workers" because they do what they are called to do so well. I hold them in high regard. I eagerly anticipate sharing their wisdom with you in this book, and I would like to thank them.

My dear husband, Joel, is super industrious. I have learned much from him. He also helped me understand the theology of work. My family has been an excellent example of Dutch diligence: my parents, Henry and Lena Kamp, and my siblings, Rich and Betty Buys, Pete and Linda VanBeek, and Henry and Teresa Kamp. My husband's family also has an excellent work ethic: Mom and Dad Beeke have gone on to be with the Lord, but stories of their lives live on. Joel's siblings have all been dedicated in their callings: Dave and Jackie Markus, John and Marie Beeke, Jim and Ruth Beeke, and Steve and Joanne Timmer. What a blessing to be surrounded by this legacy of diligence!

My husband and I have taught our children to work, and now they and their spouses, Calvin and Laura Beeke, Esther and James Engelsma, and Isaac and Lydia Epp, are teaching us in different ways.

There are others whose wisdom I have observed or tapped into over the course of many years: Laura Ash, Ralph and Margaret Buffinga, Bree Cornish, Jen DeHaan, Jim and Marie (Marie is now with the Lord) Engelsma, Marguerite Lane, Schel and Terri Paulk, Steve Renkema, Cheryl Snoek, the Julian Turnbull family, and Henry and Jackie VanderVeen.

I have another reason for writing this book. Unemployment is currently low in the United States, but I have heard stories of employers having difficulty finding good workers. One employer told me that individuals will apply for a job just to fulfill the unemployment office's requirements, without ever intending to actually take the job. Or they will work, but they lack character traits of diligence, honesty, and dedication. I sense trends in our culture in which parents feel they are being cruel to their children if they ask them to work. Then there are the stories of twenty-five- to thirty-year-olds who return to their parents' home and play video games all day. So I hope to encourage parents—to give you permission if that's what you need—to require your children to work, and to give you ideas on how to accomplish this so your children are ready to grasp adult responsibilities in society.

The rock-solid foundation of all true wisdom is the Word of God. Proverbs and Ecclesiastes are loaded with rich advice on the subject of work. I write from an American perspective, but these principles are universal. Let's be praying that God will bless our efforts to instill a strong work ethic in our dear children so they may be equipped to use their talents and follow God's calling to their vocation, all for His honor and glory.

I have blended my experiences and observations with the advice of others, I've researched books, tested them all by Scripture, and condensed them into two sections. After an introduction on the history of work, the first section is "Parental Principles," that is, Bible-based principles that form the foundation for training our children to work. They are beliefs that need to be firmly anchored in our hearts and minds before we embark on this journey of implanting a work ethic in our children. I explore the foundation and the value of God's gift of work. The second section is "Practical Principles," everyday tips and advice to approach the task with greater clarity and reachable goals. They are methods and ideas for instilling a positive and industrious atmosphere in your home while dealing with a child's resistance. At times, there is overlap between these two sections, but in the main, I have followed these divisions. In the stories I've told, some of the names are real, and some are changed.

I hope this will enable you to divide this task into manageable bites. You are busy parents, and sometimes you just need a quick shot in the arm, a bit of encouragement, or a nudge to persevere. I hope this book will convince you that we need to teach our children to work, motivate you to approach the task with energy, and encourage you to stay committed for the long haul. May God give you wisdom, strength, and blessings.

Introduction: How Work Began

God invented work. He was the first one to work. In the span of six days, His words performed the amazing work of creating the heavens and the earth and all living things. "And God saw every thing that he had made, and, behold, it was very good" (Gen. 1:31). We enjoy the work of His hands when we look all around us at the beauty of nature. His signature is on everything, from the most minute molecule we view through a microscope to the majestic mountains cloaked in snow. He still does His good and unfathomable work of sustaining this universe every moment.

We were created as human beings in God's image and likeness, which means we have some characteristics that are like His. We are to follow His example for living. In Paradise, Adam was remarkably busy. God assigned him large and essential tasks. As the highest functioning creature that God had just created, Adam was put in charge of the earth. In fact, Adam's first task was to name all the birds of the air and the beasts of the field as they passed before him (2:19).

God issued the command for man to have dominion over the earth in Genesis 1:26 and 28: "Be fruitful, and multiply, and replenish the earth, and subdue it: and have dominion over the fish of the sea, and over the fowl of the air, and over every living thing that moveth upon the earth." Eve, Adam's wife and helper, was made by God to be perfectly suitable to obey God's commands by his side.

God maintained the garden by watering the ground by a mist that went up from the earth (2:6), but He also called on Adam and Eve to "dress [work] it and to keep it" (2:15).

The Creator God put man, the creature, in charge of maintaining this vast land. First, Adam and Eve were to have children and grandchildren. Their family would fill the earth. Second, they were called to subdue the earth, to bring it under their control, and to use the natural resources for their own benefit. They were to be wise stewards and take good care of this beautiful world. Third, God told them to have dominion over the animal kingdom. As Adam and Eve looked all around at the amazing plants and animals, and as they looked up at the sun during the day and the moon and stars at night, they must have marveled at the handiwork of God and at how blessed they were to be able to rule the earth on God's behalf. All the glory belonged to God, and that brought joy and peace to Adam and Eve. Work was good—very good!

God and Adam entered into the covenant of works together, an agreement that they would be loyal to each other and meet certain conditions. Adam and Eve could freely eat of everything of the garden except for the Tree of the Knowledge of Good and Evil, and for a time, they were content with this arrangement.

Everything was perfect, peaceful, and beautiful. All that God had created was good. The food growing in the garden sustained all the living creatures. Each plant was beautiful and healthy. Adam and Eve had communion with God as they walked in the garden in the cool of the day, likely the time of evening breezes. They carried out their work as overseers of the garden, trimming the plants, harvesting the fruits, and caring for the animals. The first couple honored their Creator by fulfilling their assignments and did so with pure joy in their labors. They were surrounded by beauty, unmarred by blight, weeds, or parasites. Adam and Eve enjoyed their farming life. They slept well and had no pain or sickness. Their marriage was happy, and they looked forward to bringing children into this Paradise. There was no sin. God blessed them. Life was so good.

Work Becomes a Burden

We don't know how long the busy yet blissful existence for Adam and Eve lasted, but we know it wasn't long enough. It seems that it wasn't even long enough to fulfill God's mandate to be fruitful and multiply and replenish the earth, as Cain wasn't born yet.

We all know this saddest of all stories ever. Satan appeared in the garden as a serpent, and enticed Eve with the forbidden fruit. Eve saw its beauty. She desired knowledge she wasn't supposed to have. And so, Eve chose to eat. Adam was right there; she gave the fruit to him, and he ate it too. Immediately their eyes were opened. Guilt struck them. They were ashamed of their nakedness, so they sewed aprons of fig leaves to make their first set of clothes.

God could have struck Adam and Eve dead on the spot. The covenant of works Adam had entered into with God threatened punishment of death if they ate of the forbidden fruit. However, God showed mercy. He did not destroy our first parents, but He did mete out immediate punishment to them. Eve would have sorrow in conceiving and giving birth to children, and she would bristle under the leadership of her husband. The ground would be cursed because of their sin. The farming that was a joy before would be tedious now; Adam would sweat as he toiled against the thorns and thistles. It would be difficult to grow crops. Putting food on the table would consume most of his time. When Adam's time on earth was done, his body would return to the very ground that his sweat drops had fallen upon all his life. "For dust thou art, and unto dust shalt thou return" (Gen. 3:19).

But God did more than simply punish Adam and Eve. He also gave the promise of the coming Messiah, Jesus Christ, who would crush Satan and save mankind from sin and death. So, this very sad chapter in human history ends on a note of hope in God. Although we move on from here with sadness and burdens in our work, God is not finished working. Mixed with the punishments, the grace of God shines. The sun glistens between the clouds. Praise God for His mercy!

God Redeems Work

God created work to be good. But Adam and Eve sinned and forever changed the nature of work for themselves and for all their descendants. We, the family of Adam, are sinful, yet God remains perfect and pure and good. He is the same yesterday, today, and forever. God is still working today; His work is perfect. We work too, though our work is far from perfect. But remember, God gives many blessings in spite of the challenges.

What Is God's Work?

We look around and see evidence of God's work of creation everywhere. We exclaim with the psalmist, "The heavens declare the glory of God; and the firmament sheweth his handywork" (Ps. 19:1). The sun, moon, and stars are called to praise Him in Psalm 148, as are the elements of the weather, all animals and plants, and even the earth itself. Most of all, people are to praise the name of the Lord for His glorious creation. Daily let us look up and down, left and right, take a deep breath, see the beauty and wonder of God's creation, and thank and praise Him for it!

In His original work of creation, God built in elements that ensured living creatures were self-propagating. He didn't make a tree that would just live one hundred years and then die. He wondrously created "the fruit tree yielding fruit after his kind, whose seed is in itself" (Gen. 1:11). He gave animals and humans the ability to procreate. God is the Great Designer of all things scientific. He established the laws of nature in the realm of the physical sciences and life sciences.

Still, this world needs His omnipotence to carry on every minute. He has His hand on the day-to-day operations. This is providence. He upholds and governs the universe—the motion of celestial bodies, the makeup of all things terrestrial, the growth of plants, the change of seasons, the fluctuations of the weather, the ebb and flow of sickness and health, and the birth and life and death of man. His providence directs the events of our individual lives as well as those of the whole world. We do well to acknowledge Him, for without His providence, we would die.

God's greatest work is His work of redemption. God the Father designed a plan to save sinners from the wages of sin, which is death (Rom. 6:23). This plan of salvation required Jesus, His Son, to come to earth by way of the incarnate birth, to be born in a humble barn and be laid in a feeding trough, to be raised in a working-class family, to labor as a carpenter, to go about the land teaching the ways of God and healing the sick, to be hated and persecuted for who He was, to suffer the shameful death of the cross, and to rise again on the third day. Why? To save sinners. Jesus said, "I must work the works of him that sent me" (John 9:4).

We cannot do any work to earn salvation for ourselves or for our children. But God offers it to us. "Repent ye, and believe the gospel" (Mark 1:15). "Believe on the Lord Jesus Christ, and thou shalt be saved" (Acts 16:31). But isn't repenting and believing *work*? Yes, it is God's work in us. "For by grace are ye saved through faith; and that not of yourselves: it is the gift of God: not of works, lest any man should boast" (Eph. 2:8–9). So, God speaks to us through His Word and through preaching; the Holy Spirit awakens our heart to take heed to the Word; and we respond in faith, repenting and believing. But it is not our own work, it is the Holy Spirit moving in us. All glory be to God!

Let's ask ourselves, "Has God worked in my soul?" If He has, praise God! But if you have not experienced His salvation, cry out to Him from the bottom of your heart, "Lord, be merciful to me a sinner!" Repent and believe! Pray that God will *not* have to exercise His work of judgment against you. Ask God to convert you by the power of His Holy Spirit. Pray that the blood of Jesus, shed on the cross, will cover your sins. Seek Him until you find rest for your soul.

What Is Man's Work?

How did the fall change our work? We are still made in the image of God. God works, so we are called to work too. He draws the parallel in the fourth commandment, "Six days shalt thou labor, and do all thy work.... For in six days the LORD made heaven and earth, the sea, and all that in them is" (Ex. 20:9, 11). Work is a gift of God. He blessed each of us with abilities and talents, which give us joy and fulfillment when they are used in a profitable way. Yes, there is sweat and drudgery, but if we persevere, there are rewards in the end. God has redeemed, or bought back, the good things about work.

God's mandate to be fruitful and multiply, to replenish the earth, to subdue it, and to have dominion over the creatures still stands. What does this mean to us today?

Be Fruitful and Multiply and Replenish the Earth

We are to follow God's design for the human race to carry on, which is marriage. A man and a woman leave their parents and cleave to each other; they are one flesh. A blessed marriage is one infused with love to God first, then love to each other. Love brings with it a desire to serve. Into this union, God brings children through the wonder of conception and birth. We do the work of raising our children, teaching them to work. God wants us to replenish the earth, to spread out over the whole earth and fill it.[1]

Subdue the Earth

Wherever we live on this earth, we are to subdue it. We may use the earth for our benefit. We may farm and then eat food from plants and animals. We may use rocks, clay, wood, and metal to build our homes, mine minerals to improve our daily lives, use materials and the laws of nature to invent machines, and develop our civilization. But we may not misuse the earth or its contents. God's charge to Adam to "dress and keep" the garden of Eden directs us to be careful stewards.[2] God cares deeply about the earth He so masterfully

---

1. James M. Hamilton Jr., *Work and Our Labor in the Lord* (Wheaton, Ill.: Crossway, 2017), 19.

2. Daniel M. Doriani, *Work: Its Purpose, Dignity, and Transformation* (Phillipsburg, NJ: P&R, 2019), 26–27.

designed and created. In fact, no one cares more for the earth, not even the most fervent environmentalist. Yet we must not worship the earth itself or any part of it. We must worship God alone. When we do that, we will want to take good care of all our natural resources. We will be the best environmentalists around.

Exercise Dominion
God's charge of exercising dominion means that we represent God and rule over the animals. God is a spirit, so man, being made in God's image, is the visible, tangible presence of God on earth. Man is God's representative. Human beings are the highest functioning creatures, though animals are intricate and amazing and have instincts and capabilities we don't have. We have a soul; animals do not. God gives man permission to rule animals, but this does not mean conquer, destroy, or mistreat them. "A righteous man regardeth the life of his beast" (Prov. 12:10). To "exercise dominion" indicates Adam was to study and understand his surroundings, to work hard to figure out how to use plants and animals for his and his family's good and for God's glory.[3] Adam, the first farmer, lived 930 years and raised a large family, accumulating a vast amount of knowledge about animals and plants. Still today, we take good care of the creatures because they are created by the God we worship.

Burdens and Blessings
It is obvious that the fall has affected work today. Thorns and thistles are obstacles. Work can be extremely difficult. Sweat is part of life. Many factors hinder enjoyment in work. Poverty and poor working conditions are the plight of many around the world, especially in third-world countries. Oppressive employers can make life difficult. Insufficient wages make workers feel defeated. Millions around the world suffer from circumstances outside their control, making work

---

3. "Dominion," Answers in Genesis, accessed December 8, 2020, https://answersingenesis.org/answers-bible-curriculum/media-supplements/dominion.

burdensome. This dismal life is the only reality that many people know. Those of us who enjoy more comfort must certainly pray for and support these folks in any way possible.

Then there are some who make work burdensome for themselves. It's an attitude thing. It's a cultural thing. It's usually only found in flourishing economies. It's a complaining spirit of our day, the "Thank God it's Friday," the live for the fun attitude, and the groaning when we have to get up for work or school. Let's not buy into this. Work is a privilege. Having a job is a gift of God.

God's common grace abounds all over the world. Believers and unbelievers alike spend most of their waking hours working. Work is necessary for our very existence. In the motion of life, we are born, we eat and sleep, we move, we grow, we have relationships, and we work. The cycle of our daily lives is this: we need food and shelter, so we work, so we earn wages.

Even though God is "angry with the wicked every day" (Ps. 7:11), He still has "no pleasure in the death of the wicked; but that the wicked turn from his way and live" (Ezek. 33:11). He commands "all men every where to repent" (Acts 17:30). He graciously invites sinners to repent and believe on Him. But meanwhile, He bestows many undeserved gifts on unbelievers through His common grace. Some of those gifts include food, shelter, safety, and provision—and a paycheck. Traits of intelligence, creativity, diligence, integrity, bravery, and strength come from God. He gives many a sincere desire to do what is good and right. He equips many with compassionate and generous hearts that move them to help and serve others. He gifts some with admirable leadership skills in philanthropy, business, and science, which results in improving the lives of many people. God gives unbelievers joy and fulfillment in their work.

But no matter how many blessings of common grace an unbeliever experiences, the life of a believer is more fulfilling. It is deeper and more joyful. Even a painful, trial-filled existence of a believer is better than a comfortable, trouble-free life of an unbeliever.

When God is honored, we Christians feel deeply fulfilled. Scripture outlines four principles relating to work.[4] First, all honorable work is sacred. It doesn't matter whether we clean toilets or run a multinational company, if we are diligent and work honestly, then we honor God and God honors that work. Everything we do is in the presence of God, so it is religious and holy (Eph. 6:5–9).

Second, God calls every person to their work. He equips each of us with talents, and He requires us to use these gifts fully. Thankfully, we usually enjoy what we are good at, so the side benefit of joy is a blessing from God as well. We are grateful to God for our talents, and again, we express honor and gratitude to Him (Matt. 25:14–30).

Third, we are to be devoted to our work, but not enslaved by it. It's a blessing to be diligent and dedicated, but we must balance work with the spiritual, emotional, mental, and physical lives of ourselves and our families (1 Cor. 10:31).

Love of God overflows to love for our neighbor, so the fourth principle is service. Serving God and others is to be our prime motivation and goal of our work. This can be direct service, as in ministry or medical occupations, or indirectly, as in building homes or manufacturing cars. This is a heart thing. It's living out the Golden Rule. As Jesus says, "Therefore all things whatsoever ye would that men should do to you, do ye even so to them" (Matt. 7:12). Two people may be doing the same work with different motives. The HVAC tech who fixes your furnace in a blizzard because he cares that you are warm is honoring God more than the tech who is happy he gets paid extra for an after-hours call (Mark 12:29–31).

In conclusion, work is good, even in a sinful world. God works, and He blesses our work. Jesus was a carpenter. He honored shepherds by calling Himself the Great Shepherd. He called His disciples to become "fishers of men." He said, "My Father worketh hitherto [until now], and I work" (John 5:17). As image-bearers of God, let's

---

4. James W. Beeke, *Bible Doctrine for Teens and Young Adults,* vol. 3 (Grand Rapids: Eerdmans, 1990), 94–97.

honor Him by following His example. Whatever our work is, let's pray, "And let the beauty of the LORD our God be upon us: and establish thou the work of our hands upon us; yea, the work of our hands establish thou it" (Ps. 90:17).

PART 1
Parental Principles

Chapter 1

Work Is Good for Kids

Recently, our daughter, who is married and the mother of three small children, read a blog on motherhood. A young mom questioned, "Should I unload the dishwasher while my daughter is awake? Or should I only play with her?" A prevailing attitude today is that the best parenting is to play, either educational play or fun play, with our children during all their waking hours. To require children to work at a young age would be cruel, the epitome of "child labor"!

I would hasten to disagree. Work is good for kids! There are many benefits, though we do need to be wary of overworking our children. When children are included in the family's work, they are included in the activities of the family. They have a sense of being needed and valued, which makes them feel worthwhile and happy. Additionally, work teaches life skills. Children learn obedience and self-discipline. Young children see work as fun. Work is a wise use of time and gives families together time. It is honorable to work.

Play Is Valuable

"Play is the work of the child," said Maria Montessori, founder of a philosophy of education taught in the schools named after her. Though I don't endorse all her beliefs, I would agree with this statement. She believed play promotes healthy "development of a child's fine and gross motor skills, language, socialization, personal awareness, emotional well-being, creativity, problem-solving, and learning ability."[1]

Play comes naturally to children. They learn about their environment and about themselves through play. In the sandbox, Abigail pats mud into pies, while Jamison uses his bulldozer to build roads around a lake. Later, Zoey "reads" a story to her doll. William builds a tower with blocks, then knocks it down. Our little ones spend most of their waking hours playing. Play is wonderful!

The Bible describes children playing in the ideal, restored Jerusalem: "And the streets of the city shall be full of boys and girls playing in the streets thereof" (Zech. 8:5). In 1 Corinthians 13:11, Paul says that when he was a child, he spoke, understood, and thought as a child, but when he became a man, he put away childish things.

The Transition to Work

We all agree that children play. We all agree that adults work. So, how do we get from one to the other? It's a process. Through their growing up years, children start out with mostly play. As the years go by, the playtime decreases, and the work time increases, until adulthood, when the bulk of our waking hours are spent working. How do we find that balance? What is appropriate for each age? Let's consider several factors.

First, learning takes place in a progressive, incremental manner. Work is learned over time and with practice. If we parents do all the work around the house and require none from our children, and if the only work they do is at school, there will be two results. When they enter the work world at sixteen or eighteen or twenty-two years of age, they will lack many basic skills, such as cleaning up their own messes, preparing food, and fixing things. Furthermore, they will expect others to do menial tasks for them. If they get married,

---

1. "'Play Is the Work of the Child,' Maria Montessori," Child Development Institute, accessed December 8, 2020, https://childdevelopmentinfo.com/child-development/play-work-of-children/#gs.4r9p30.

they will be in for a shock—or their spouse will be! They won't be equipped to either support or run a household.

On the contrary, we are to "train up a child in the way he should go: and when he is old, he will not depart from it" (Prov. 22:6). An age-old axiom is, "Give me a child for the first seven years, and I will give you the man." The most important learning takes place in those early years. Foundational skills, like communicating and interacting with others, personal hygiene, manners, and basic physics of how things work together, are learned. If life is mostly play and little work, children will be upset when the time comes when they have to do "real work" like washing walls and cleaning the garage. It is much better to have work be a part of their very earliest memories so that it is built in their minds that work is part of life.

Farm kids are proof that work is good for kids. They learn how to care for animals, grow and harvest food, fix equipment, and buy and sell their products. Beyond that, they build habits of perseverance, diligence, concentration, and working for a goal. Those habits are just as important as the specific skills themselves because they can be applied to any situation. If a child learns to problem solve next to his father while fixing a lawn mower, he may apply that quality to his job as an engineer as an adult. We can't all be farm kids, but if your child has an opportunity for a weekend or summer job on the farm, go for it! It will be great for them. Proverbs 10:5 describes the farm boy, but it can be applied to any child: "He that gathereth in summer is a wise son: but he that sleepeth in harvest is a son that causeth shame."

Friends of ours own a flower business. They began years ago in their garage, and they've always worked hard for long hours. Their greatest challenge today is finding reliable employees who will consistently put in an honest and wholehearted day's labor and who won't try to weasel out of work while complaining about wages and benefits.

Let's challenge ourselves to raise our children to be good workers someday. To do that, we must start now. Let's embark on this adventure!

Chapter 2

Foundations

One Sunday evening after church, we had the dad of a large family over, with six of his children, for coffee. The kids were in their teens and twenties, all preparing diligently for future careers. I asked him what he and his wife had done to instill a work ethic in their children. He gave an interesting answer. "We memorized the Westminster Shorter Catechism with them." I asked him to explain the connection. "Well, we figured if they had biblical doctrines firmly settled in their minds, then everything else would be built on that foundation. My wife taught them many Bible passages as well. And we prayed God would bring it home to their hearts."

We want the house we live in to have a strong and sure foundation so that it endures. The foundation of our children's lives must also be strong and sure in order to uphold them. The principles we teach our children when they are young will have a lifelong impact on their work as well as their entire being. Whether we are intentional about instilling those principles or are just raising our children haphazardly, they *are* learning principles. The only reliable source of the building blocks of the foundation of our children's lives is Scripture. If we want our children to have a good work ethic, certain biblical principles must be written on their hearts and minds and woven into their actions and habits. Let's look at them.

Truth

Christians all want truth. We want to live according to truth. Where can we find truth? Simply, in God's Word. Everything we teach our children must be according to Scripture. God is truth personified. Jesus said to the Jews who believed in Him, "If ye continue in my word, then are ye my disciples indeed; and ye shall know the truth, and the truth shall make you free" (John 8:31–32).

We want our children to be truth-tellers. Honesty is a trait we monitor closely. We test our children's words. Do they sound believable? Are they describing what really happened? Are our children owning up to their misdeeds? Every child is born with a conscience, but each one is a sinner also. They test out truth. Most children will tell lies at some point. One of our children went through two stages of telling tall tales. In fact, much of what that child said during those times didn't pass the truth test. But we kept working and praying, and eventually things changed. We do our children a favor to catch them and sort out the truth. Instruction may cure them, but we shouldn't hesitate to discipline if lying continues. The younger they learn to tell the truth, the better.

From honesty flows integrity, which is behaving uprightly according to moral standards of right and wrong. These traits are caught as much as they are taught. "The just man walketh in his integrity: his children are blessed after him" (Prov. 20:7). Children are very perceptive at detecting our inconsistencies, and those little eyes are watching all the time. If the cashier gives us too much change back, and we return it, our children learn that doing the right thing is more important than having extra money. And God's blessing rests upon upright behavior.

As our children grow up, they develop a reputation for themselves. "Even a child is known by his doings, whether his work be pure, and whether it be right" (Prov. 20:11). We as parents have a huge influence in developing their honesty, integrity, and faithfulness. Heart-to-heart discussions during family worship about how the motives of our hearts impact our words and actions can help children understand themselves. And candid talks with our children individually about their own words and behaviors, good and bad, can help them develop integrity. A combination of high expectations, love, affirmation, and judiciously used discipline will nurture these beautiful traits that will place them in good stead in their future work life and relationships.

My father is a man of few words but is filled with integrity. My sister gave him a plaque once that read:

> Your talk talks,
> And your walk talks,
> But your walk talks more than your talk talks.

Soli Deo Gloria

Once we have established that God is the source of all truth and that He is the Creator and Giver of all that we have and all that we are, then it naturally follows that we glorify Him. "Whether therefore ye eat, or drink, or whatsoever ye do, do all to the glory of God" (1 Cor. 10:31). Are we demonstrating that the glory of God is everything to us? If we are motivated to excel for the recognition we receive, our priorities are misplaced, and our children will likely follow our example. If we get more upset when our name is smeared than when God is dishonored, we are setting our sights too low. We are looking in the mirror too much and looking into the heavens too little. As parents, we must have God's honor as our very highest longing. Our children must see and feel and know we are filled with joy when our work brings glory to God. They must see our excitement especially when sinners are saved, when righteousness is exalted, and when God is praised.

Striving for God's glory is more than just a goal or a feeling, though. We can only truly glorify God if we are saved. "Whatsoever is not of faith is sin" (Rom. 14:23). So, as parents, we must make our calling and election sure. And we must bring the gospel to our covenant children. None of us can assume we are saved by being born into a Christian family. Each of us needs to be born again and have a personal saving relationship with God. We need to repent of our sins and believe on Jesus Christ, by the power of the Holy Spirit.

Love to God

When God is our Lord and Savior, our hearts are overflowing with gratitude to God for His great salvation. Gratitude and humility live in the same heart. We know we don't deserve God's blessings, so we are thankful for them. A grateful heart sings praise to God and is happy to fulfill Micah 6:8, "He hath shewed thee, O man, what is good; and what doth the LORD require of thee, but to do justly, and to love mercy, and to walk humbly with thy God?" When we know the Lord, we want to fulfill the greatest commandment to love God above all. A worker with these characteristics will faithfully serve as an employee or an employer. "The fear of the LORD is the beginning of knowledge" (Prov. 1:7).

Love to Neighbor

Love to God, the greatest commandment, naturally overflows to love to our neighbor, which is the second greatest commandment. What does love to our neighbor look like in everyday clothes?

Kindness and Goodness

First, it looks like kindness and goodness. Home is where we spend most of our time. Family is whom we spend most of our time with. We love our family the most. We have many good times together, but sadly, we take out our frustrations the most on our siblings, parents, and children. We restrain ourselves with friends and acquaintances, yet we save our anger and unkind words for those we are closest to. This is one of those ugly realities of our sinful human nature.

So, home is the best training ground to teach kindness and goodness because we need it there the most. Kindness is the inclination of the heart to show compassion and to help others, to be gentle, loving, and considerate. Goodness is putting those inclinations into action. Some children are born kind; the rest need to be taught. Our own example—our tone of voice, the words we speak, and our actions— sets the tone of the home, which our children will likely emulate. The more love we show, the less space there is for the negatives. Praise is important. When Liam shares his Legos with his sister, recognize his generosity and affirm him. This will reinforce this behavior.

If one child consistently picks on or teases another, it must be addressed. Is there an underlying cause, such as insecurity or anger? Get to the bottom of what is going on inside. The teasing child might not realize the pain they are inflicting and might just need to learn empathy. But if cruelty is lurking in the heart, more drastic measures are called for, maybe even pastoral help. But it *must* be dealt with until it is eradicated.

Mercy and Grace

Just as mercy and grace are foundational for our spiritual life, they are interwoven into our everyday life. Sometimes when our children would argue, we would replay the scenario and discuss the direction their words *should* have taken. We would ascertain who had done wrong and require that child to say, "I'm sorry"; the other child had to say, "I forgive you." They hugged, and it was over. Did they always sincerely mean their words? No, but we were training their hearts to feel remorse and to forgive. We prayed that this would help lay the foundation for the Holy Spirit to work in their hearts to repent to God and to receive His forgiveness. At times when we were too harsh in our parenting, we apologized and asked for their forgiveness. This restored peace and goodwill.

In the course of our daily lives, we can teach our children to serve each other, to be generous and patient with each other, and to walk humbly with each other. When a sibling is sick, we pray for them and bring them soup or toast. We give gifts and share the joy of birthdays and special occasions. We help each other with homework. We do yardwork and housework together. We work together, we play together, we cry and laugh together. "Bear ye one another's burdens, and so fulfil the law of Christ" (Gal. 6:2).

Wisdom

Godly wisdom is a beautiful thing, especially when we see it in our children. Wisdom is the good use of knowledge. It shows itself by being willing to learn, be corrected, and accept counsel of others (Prov. 1:5). Wisdom follows God's commandments and searches for more wisdom (Prov. 2:1–5). The wise child has peace, joy, and wealth beyond money (Prov. 3:13–18). Foolishness leads to shame, but wisdom brings honor (Prov. 3:35; 12:8). A wise person loves what is good and hates what is evil (Prov. 8:13–14). This is just the tip of the iceberg! Read Proverbs with your children, mine the gold from its pages, and pray it will sink deeply into their hearts. "Wisdom is the principal thing; therefore get wisdom: and with all thy getting get understanding" (Prov. 4:7). Most of all, Jesus is Wisdom; when we find Him, we find life (Prov. 8:35).

Holiness

God wouldn't be God if He weren't holy. If we love God, we will love what He loves, which is holiness and purity. David said, "Oh how love I thy law! it is my meditation all the day" (Ps. 119:97). The law of the Lord must be the law of our households, infused with a whole lot of love. "Follow peace with all men, and holiness, without which no man shall see the Lord" (Heb. 12:14). We want to be pure, and we grieve when we are not. We want our children to be pure, and we grieve when they are not. We pray. We take our sins to the foot of the cross, and we pray that Jesus's blood shed on the cross will cleanse us. We pray, "Lord, convert us and convert our dear children!" Then, and only then, can we be righteous and good, only through Jesus.

Conclusion

If we want to rear our children with a good work ethic, we need to aim for more than superficial behavior. Our foundation must be built on the solid Rock, Jesus Christ, and on His teachings. It must be woven through our every thought, action, and word. We need to teach our precious children the truth of Scripture, that all of life is to be to God's glory, to love God above all and our neighbor as ourselves, and to love what is good and holy. Just as the parents brought their children to Jesus for His blessing, so today, we can do the same! He laid His hands on them and blessed them and said, "Suffer the little children to come unto me, and forbid them not: for of such is the kingdom of God" (Mark 10:14). God entrusts us with our children, but He doesn't leave us on our own. "I can do all things through Christ which strengtheneth me" (Phil. 4:13).

Chapter 3

It's in the Atmosphere

Our children are a gift from God to us. They are our greatest treasure. We can't take our earthly treasures and possessions to heaven with us, but we can take our children. That is why we plead on God's covenant promises, that He would save us and them. Then we can spend eternity together. So, while we are living here on earth together, spiritual training and prayer are our top priorities. But training for everyday life is vital too. In fact, they are intertwined. The foundations we discussed in chapter 2 have implications for both. "Blessed is every one that feareth the LORD; that walketh in his ways. For thou shalt eat the labour of thine hands: happy shalt thou be, and it shall be well with thee" (Ps. 128:1–2).

There is more. Through my observations of and interviews with families who seem to have a balanced approach to rearing children with interpersonal and work skills and have trained their children to be responsible and independent, I have noticed some common attitudes. I've seen something that begins in the heart and shows itself in their behavior. Love, encouragement, expectation, and example are the attitudes in the atmosphere of their homes.

Some of you are groaning with guilt at this moment. I am too. We fall short of these ideals, past or present. But I want to encourage us. God's grace covers a multitude of sins. He is in the business of redemption—in both the spiritual and natural realms. He can take our everyday mistakes and use them for good. Romans 8:28 encourages us: "All things work together for good to them that love God, to them who are the called according to his purpose." In Joel 2, the prophet warns Judah that terrible destruction is coming because the people are so sinful. He invites them to repent, then he describes how they can expect that God will restore them physically and spiritually: "And I will restore to you the years that the locust hath eaten" (v. 25). We can pray that God will restore us and our children as well. Keep praying. "Before they call, I will answer," God says (Isa. 65:24). God can answer prayers retroactively. Hope in the Lord!

Love and Encouragement

Let's turn our attention in this chapter more to everyday life. We discussed God's greatest commandments, to love God above all and to love our neighbor as ourselves. Our family is our closest neighbor. We love them the most. Our greatest joys and our worst fears center on them. We want the best for them. We care about other people's kids, but we care the most about our own. We are empathetic with the burdens of other families, but our heartache is the worst if something bad happens to our own children. Somehow, our greatest frustrations come from our children as well. In fact, our love gets tested. Or maybe we would say there are days when we don't *like* them so much. When Caleb screams in the grocery cart that he needs that ball and you can't calm him down no matter what, or when Hilda has refused to clean her room for weeks and narrows her eyes at you and says, "Get out of my space," somehow the love is a little harder to find.

But I want to shout something to all parents: *"Keep the love in your heart!"* Whatever it takes—talking to God, talking to your spouse, talking to yourself, reading a God-centered book, meditating on Scripture, going for a run, lifting weights, looking at your child's baby picture, or a combination of any of these, find that love back and hang onto it. Even in the hard times, love must drive our discipline. Love must guide our words and our reactions. Tough love at times? Yes, by all means. But love, nonetheless. Keep the love in your heart!

Love in our hearts will ensure love is in the atmosphere of our homes. How do we get that? By following God's advice in Ephesians 6:4, "And, ye fathers, provoke not your children to wrath: but bring them up in the nurture and admonition of the Lord." First, Paul tells us not to make our children angry by our parenting techniques. Provoking happens in a variety of ways: by being harsh, overly strict or severe, angry, sarcastic, insulting, cruel, evil, abusive, unfair, unreasonable, or overbearing.

Instead, we are to nurture our children. We care for their physical, emotional, mental, moral, and spiritual needs. Compassion is in the mix. We want the best for them. Our goal for them is to grow up to be well-rounded individuals. We educate them for adult life, we nourish their bodies with nutritious food, and we train them in righteousness. When they feel our love, they are far more inclined to obey and to work for the good of the family.

We also need to admonish them in the Lord. We affirm good behavior, and we correct them with love when they do wrong. We instruct and explain with words. At times, discipline is needed. This is done in the spirit of Christ in Revelation 3:19, "As many as I love, I rebuke and chasten." It's not pleasant for the parent or the child, but it's necessary for correction, and it's for their profit in the end.

How do we nurture this love in our own hearts so we can properly nurture our children? Starting out the day with personal devotions sets the tone of our hearts. Memorizing verses can strengthen us. If things get tense, send up little prayers: "Lord, give me wisdom." Try to empathize with your child. It's possible they are bothered about something else but take their frustrations out on us. Instead of letting our emotions escalate, try asking in a kind voice, "It seems like something is bothering you. Anything I can do to help?" "A soft answer turneth away wrath" (Prov. 15:1). It might touch them, and they may open up to us.

Affection is so important for showing love—affection between husband and wife makes the children feel secure, and affection between parents and children makes everyone feel loved. Affection can diffuse a tense situation, though wisdom is needed because it can aggravate a child also.

Our words impact our children greatly. An encouraging comment can give hope and cheer when they are down. God is the great encourager of His children; our children depend on our encouragement as well. Words of Scripture and words of wisdom and kindness can give them strength to go on in their work. One of our children would say in moments of being upset, "Just tell me everything is going to be okay!" So that's what I learned to do. It actually calmed me down too because I thought of Romans 8:28, the "all things work together for good" verse. I was telling the truth, though there might be pain along the way. If our child is overwhelmed with a task and can't see their way through, say a gentle word, "You made it through last week's tough lesson. I know you can do it again." Encouragement lets our children know we are on their side and that we will get through this together.

Sometimes we need to chill a bit. Instead of responding to resistance with irritation, we can say the same words in a pleasant, positive tone of voice. Sophia gripes, "I don't want to pull weeds!" You respond calmly, "Well, we are going after those weeds, and the garden will look great when we finish. So, let's go!"—just a straightforward answer, emotion not needed. Even humor can diffuse a situation. If they spread food all over the place while baking with you, take a picture and laugh at the mess (it's better than crying), then get busy cleaning it up together. "Keep calm and carry on."[1]

If their behavior requires discipline and you are angry inside, say, "I will talk with you in fifteen minutes." It gives them a few moments

---

1. The British government displayed this slogan on posters in 1939, as they faced WWII and potential air raids, to motivate and boost the morale of the citizens. It's a useful slogan to keep the peace in our homes today.

to reflect (and hopefully repent) and gives you time to decide on a wise response with a profitable goal. Do what it takes to prevent words you regret—imagine duct tape over your mouth, go to your bedroom and pray hard. I was always thankful for days that lasted only twenty-four hours and for God's providence that our children sleep eight to twelve of those hours. Every night, but especially after a challenging day, I would go look at that most beautiful sight of our sleeping children, and feel the love reset button in my heart being pushed. Then I would go get some sleep myself and pray for a better day tomorrow.

Example and Expectation

Of all the parents I interviewed, the most common answer to the question "How do you get your kids to work?" was "By example." When I asked some of the kids of diligent parents what their take was on that, they replied, "We knew Dad was working so hard at his job every day; we didn't want to disappoint him. We knew he was working hard to support us, so we had to do our part by working hard at home with Mom."

I asked one of those couples what they did when their children resisted work or acted lazy. They paused and said, "I don't know if we were just blessed with diligent kids, but we didn't have too much trouble. We just worked, and we expected them to work with us, and they did. We didn't really have hard-and-fast rules; we just worked as a family. Like on a Saturday, we all did yard work together. Everything we asked them to do, we did with them. They saw that menial work wasn't below our dignity. When they were old enough and proficient at a job, they would do it on their own. But we continue to do many things together as a family."

We went to a conference in Canada years ago, where we met a retired sociologist. He told us something intriguing: "Of all the immigrant groups I have studied, there are none like the Dutch Canadians, who were so successful in business and had cohesive families." He attributed it to their diligence and dedication to family, church, and school. But most of all, he saw it as God's blessing on these character traits.

It's in the atmosphere. It's pervasive. When parents lead by example and include their children in as much work as possible around the house, then there is an expectation that the children pick up that imbeds this principle in their minds: "A big part of life is work. That's just the way it is, and that's fine."

There is more to this atmosphere. I've seen a key attitude in the parents who have had the least trouble with instilling a work ethic in their children. I know some of them very well, and they have a no-nonsense principle planted firmly in their own hearts. It's this: "I work. Our kids work. If they object, I nip it in the bud, and we get on with our work." No tolerance for resistance. Children sense if there is room for negotiation. The not-so-diligent child finds that tiny crack in the wall and tries to drive a wedge between Mom and Dad in order to find an excuse for not working. But if both parents present a united front, there are no cracks. The sooner our children realize there is no way out of the work, the sooner they accept it and get to work, and the more content and obedient they are. We need to show authority, mixed with love and care, without being authoritarian.

Finally, let's not look at this as a life of toil and trials. Yes, some people have difficult, burdensome work they are called to do. But for most of us, we can control our attitude about work. Let's not adopt the world's negative attitude toward it. Instead, let's see work as the gift of God that it is. Let's get excited about work and what we can discover and learn. Let's love work and expect our kids to also. Let's show our joy and sense of reward and accomplishment in our work and then pass on that positive attitude to our children.

Chapter 4

Subdue Their Will to Set Them Free

When I was a young mother, a dear sweet friend, a mother of ten, told me, "A child's will needs to be made submissive to the parents. Usually between the ages of eighteen to thirty months, every child will have a blowout encounter with Mom or Dad. And the parent *has to win*. If that happens, things will be smoother afterward. If the child wins, the confrontations will continue. The older the child is, the harder it is for the parent to win." One of our children picked a day when a famous theologian was visiting for lunch to have that battle. I remember it clearly. Thankfully, lunch was over, and my husband quickly escorted our guest out the door. Did I win? I think by a hair.

But it's not about us winning; it's about our child obeying. It's about subduing their will so that they can be trained and can be freed from selfishness to realize their potential. God commands our children, "Honour thy father and thy mother: that thy days may be long upon the land which the LORD thy God giveth thee" (Ex. 20:12). They need to learn to obey you so that they will obey other figures of authority—teachers, future employers, and God Himself.

God loans us our children, and we are to train them according to His precepts. He places us in authority over them. We represent God in our homes. We honor God when we train our children to honor Him. It is our responsibility to love them, nurture them, and because they are sinners, to admonish them. It's not an easy task. We need wisdom from sources outside ourselves to know what to do. Trustworthy sources include Scripture above all, advice from wise family and friends, and answers to prayer.

Start Young

I believe that training the will starts in infancy. If we respond to every little peep our baby makes, they will soon learn that they will be fed or cuddled whenever they cry out. And then the intervals of calmness will become shorter. But if we feed them on somewhat of a schedule and hold and cuddle them sufficiently, then it is good for them to cry sometimes. It expands their lungs; it's like exercise. Talking and singing to them as well as pacifiers, swings, rockers, and toys are helpful to distract them. We *can* teach them patience. And we *can* teach them that we won't give them everything they want the moment they want it.

As babies grow and move around, they are able to get into trouble—touching things that could hurt them, going to dangerous places like stairways, and putting harmful things in their mouths. None of us would allow this, so we shout, "No!" and take measures to protect them from themselves. This is training the will.

Appropriate discipline is called for, especially when they show anger or defiance. And yes, even babies and toddlers *can* do this. When a very young child shows these innate emotions, a firm reprimand, a stern stare, a shake of your head while you firmly hold him or her will convey a message. A child's scowling "No!" to mom or dad must be dealt with. When your child gets older and the defiance is clearly from a rebellious heart, then decisive discipline is called for until that behavior is totally eradicated. Zero tolerance for defiance. Do not laugh or take pictures or give any indication whatsoever that you think they are cute or funny, which only positively reinforces negative behavior. If you need any incentive to deal with defiance firmly and immediately, just picture your child as a sixteen-year-old behaving the same way.

It Has to Be Done

A crucial underlying principle to remember when we rear our children is that *they are sinners*. They are sinners because we bore them, and we are sinners. We love them from the bottom of our hearts. But they need to be trained by us, and they need to be saved by Jesus. So, we shouldn't be surprised when our little darling sins. In fact, we should expect it and be ready to respond when it happens. "Foolishness is bound in the heart of a child; but the rod of correction shall drive it far from him" (Prov. 22:15).

A horse needs to be broken in so it can be ridden. Then it is useful. It can serve a purpose instead of bucking wildly and being a danger to itself and those around it. I read that a horse will be more loyal and more enjoyable if they are broken to follow their leader out of respect instead of fear.[1] Aren't children the same? By chastising firmly but with love in our hearts, following biblical principles, we gradually bend our child's will to be submissive to God's will. When they feel our love, when we encourage them, when we affirm them for doing right, when they know we want what is best for them, they will come around to submission. They will be content. It might be a long process, but if we persevere, God will bless it (Prov. 8:32).

We need to subdue their will but not break their spirit. Paul warns us that when we provoke our children to anger, they will be discouraged (Col. 3:21). Their spirits will be broken. Without encouragement mixed with the correction, they will feel like they can't do anything right. They will feel picked on. If we are constantly negative, a time will come when they will tune us out. When they make mistakes, they will feel like an abysmal failure; they won't pick themselves up and try again. They won't get excited about learning or working or obeying. They might rebel against us or take out their frustrations on someone younger and smaller, resulting in bullying.

---

1. Ryan Corrigan, "How to Break a Horse," WikiHow, updated July 14, 2020, https://www.wikihow.com/Break-a-Horse.

Friends of ours have adopted multiple children from various backgrounds. One child suffered from detachment syndrome and fetal alcohol syndrome. As a toddler, she would rage for hours. Her mom would hold her tightly, rock her, and calmly tell her she loved her over and over and that she must not act in this way. I call this a "loving straitjacket." Thankfully, most of us don't have to deal with such an extreme situation, but some of us have little children who throw temper tantrums. The loving straitjacket is a useful tool to bring peace to our child and to keep ourselves calm in the storm as well.

All children are different. I was in the back corner of the grocery store a while ago when I heard high-pitched crying. As I made my way to the checkout lane, the noise grew louder. I tried not to stare, but I couldn't help but see a girl, about four years old, lying on the floor, kicking and flailing her arms. She kept screaming, "I want that doll!" She shook with rage. Tears streamed out of her bulging eyes and down her red cheeks. Her mother finished her business quickly, picked up her daughter, and pushed the cart along. The girl kicked and hit her mother and kept crying and screaming. Mom did not give in. The girl did not get the doll. She was not happy at all.

Another time I was in the store waiting in line. A child ahead of me wanted some candy. Mom said no. The little boy looked very sad, put his head down, and shed a few tears. But a few minutes later, he calmly snuggled up to her. He was content.

What was the difference between these two children (aside from their personalities)? Both wanted something badly. Both moms said no. The girl could only think about what she wanted. She had not learned to submit to her mom. She was so angry things didn't go her way that she didn't care if she screamed at her mom and caused a commotion. She couldn't see her mother's love beyond her mother's no. The boy knew that the chocolate wasn't going to be melting in his mouth anytime soon. It made him sad, but he accepted it because he had to obey. He went to his mom for comfort because he knew she loved him. Which child was more content? Of course, the little boy.

He knew he had to accept the circumstances, and he moved on. The girl kept screaming.

What about the strong-willed child? Everything in this book applies to the strong-willed child—just double or triple the intensity. All children need love and affirmation mixed with guidance and admonition, but you might need to be more intentional and creative with your strong-willed child. You will be tested more, you will be exasperated more, and your efforts will seem like they are wasted. But just like sailing a ship through a storm, stay calm, keep your hand on the wheel and your eye on the goal, and keep praying. Stay away from the rocks to prevent shipwreck. Expect high waves and deep swells. The strong-willed child often has special talents and intelligence, as well as strong desires and drive. They can be self-centered and so much in tune with their own thoughts and wishes that they run roughshod over the rest of the family. Show much love with the correction. Consistency is key. Don't let them make you dizzy with their circular arguments. Think hard about what you require of them, communicate it clearly, and stick to your guns. Channel their strengths toward profitable skills, and give them independence (safely) in as many areas as possible so that they have some control over their lives.

How do we know if we have succeeded in subduing our child's will? When they are obedient most of the time, when they are improving, and when they are not being demanding or defiant. This doesn't mean there won't be flare-ups. Child rearing is an eighteen-year or more endeavor. Though there may be a watershed moment in which they realize they need to submit to Mom and Dad, there will be many other moments of testing their will against ours. So, enjoy the adventure, worry less and pray more, love those little ones with all your heart, and steer them in the right direction. Remember that when their will is subdued, they are more content, they are released from self-defeating native impulses, and they are set free to fulfill their God-given gifts and potential.

Chapter 5

Turn Over the Reins

Once we have subdued our child's will without breaking their spirit, we have laid a foundation for the rest of their work life to be built on. When they are young, they are restrained by *parent*-discipline. Over the course of about eighteen years, they take over and become *self*-disciplined. We train and control them by our words and actions, by our love and admonishment, and by our example and instruction so that self-control is built into their character. We expect them to respect us as their parents, and we pray they will grow in character and measure up to their own standards so that they can build self-respect. It's all a long, gradual process.

The wise person with self-control is strong. According to Proverbs 16:32, "He that is slow to anger is better than the mighty; and he that ruleth his spirit than he that taketh a city." On the other hand, "He that hath no rule over his own spirit is like a city that is broken down, and without walls" (Prov. 25:28). Which verse do you want to describe your child's life? Where does each lead to? Imagine the first picture: a young person in control of their inner impulses, holding down a job, involved in positive relationships, and being a contributing member to society. Picture the second verse: a young person giving in to inner impulses, addicted to substances or porn, burning relationship bridges, and working for a paycheck but not fulfilling their potential.

Inner character is so important. When we rear our children to bring their impulses under control, we are not imprisoning them. We are not cruelly restricting their free spirit. Rather, we are freeing them to fulfill their full potential. Instead of screaming, "I want…!" they are taught the joy of sharing. Instead of lashing out at their siblings, they are restrained and taught to be kind. Instead of being bound by their selfish desires, they are set free to serve others. Then their world becomes vast and exciting because it's not all about big, little *me*. Their eyes are opened to explore the gifts God has given them.

We parents know our children very well. Let's focus on their strengths and work to develop their talents toward a viable occupation, self-sufficiency, and independence. Let's keep our eye on exciting possibilities for their future. Of course, there will be speed bumps on the way. Our children may resist what is good for them. We'll have to do many midcourse corrections, but if we anticipate changes, it won't throw us for a loop. We adjust and move on. Keep calm and carry on. Let's not lose sight of their potential.

How do we foster this transition from parent-discipline to self-discipline? Are you ready to stay in this for the long haul? I hope so, because perseverance is needed. Each child is different, so we train them in a way that suits their character. I hope to address this in the next chapter. But there are some general guidelines that apply to all children: keep it positive, build skills and habits, build confidence and independence, and build identity.

Keep It Positive

Remember Paul's advice to rear our children in the nurture and admonition of the Lord (Eph. 6:4). Every so often, ask yourself and discuss with your spouse, "Are we finding the right balance between these two? Are we addressing sin while still showing love? Are we balancing discipline with encouragement? Are we being more positive than negative? Are we enjoying our children, or are we burdened?" Don't ask these questions late in the evening after a rough day. Instead, ask them when the sun is shining after you have had a good night's sleep. I hope you will be encouraged or that you can find encouragement from God and others. "The joy of the LORD is your strength" (Neh. 8:10) is a precious verse I wish I had discovered when our children were young because it gave me such encouragement when I did notice it. I pray it will give you strength, courage, joy, and peace too.

The only way to find joy in the Lord is to walk closely with Him. Starting your day with Him in doing devotions and prayer sets you on the right foot. It literally gives you strength! Devotions with your children sets the tone for that day. When our children were young, we rotated reading through Psalms, Proverbs, Ecclesiastes, the Gospels, and James at breakfast time, but we mostly read Proverbs. It was like strapping on our tools for the day's work. I love wisdom, and not only did I crave more wisdom but I wanted desperately for our children to be wise. Proverbs is so practical for everyday life.

I know there are times when positivity seems like an impossibility. As moms, you might struggle with PMS. Everybody has bad days. Life can be hard. Kids can shred our good mood in a moment. I hear you. First, pray! Pray God's promises back to Him. "Call upon me in the day of trouble: I will deliver thee, and thou shalt glorify me" (Ps. 50:15). My favorite and frequent prayer has always been, "Lord, help me" (Matt. 15:25). It covers everything! Sometimes He gives big help, while sometimes He allows us to hang on by our fingertips. But if we are believers, He is always present with us. "I will never leave thee, nor forsake thee" (Heb. 13:5).

We can pray practical prayers too. "Set a watch, O LORD, before my mouth; keep the door of my lips" (Ps. 141:3). Ask God to help you remain calm, to react to the children wisely, and to speak or act in ways you will not regret. Sometimes I would escape into the bathroom, pray, and look into the mirror and admonish or encourage myself, saying, "You can make it till supper!" or "Smile!" Fake it if you must, or pretend you are someone else who is calmer—it's better than blowing up. I found this useful when our kids greeted work with a chorus of whining. Instead of showing my aggravation, I tried to answer in a pleasant voice, "Just think how happy you'll be when the toilets are all clean." At least hold negative words until you've had time to ponder whether to say them. You might literally try holding your hand over your mouth. "A fool uttereth all his mind: but a wise man keepeth it in till afterwards" (Prov. 29:11). Positivity and negativity are like dominoes. If we answer negative comments with more negative, it only gets worse. But if we can put a positive spin on a stressful situation, we can calm things down.

If we parents look at work in a positive light, our children will pick up the same attitude. Our niece, a mom of four, makes work fun by being cheerful and by working together as a family. For instance, every Saturday morning they sit in a circle and have a clothes-folding party, challenging each other to see if they can get the pile folded in seven minutes. They clean the house together and celebrate afterward by playing outside.

One amazingly easy way to pass on positivity to little children is to praise them for the little jobs they do. Our daughter claps and cheers when her little children finish a task. When I babysit and we finish washing dishes or folding clothes, our granddaughter shouts triumphantly, "We did it!" Everybody loves a celebration.

Adults and children alike also love to be appreciated. We husbands and wives enjoy being recognized and thanked for our daily work, even though it's expected of us. The same goes for our children. When they work, they help us, so thanking them is genuine. It makes them feel valued because they are filling a purpose and contributing to the running of the household. Expressing gratitude is a way to humbly serve each other and to nurture a sense of gratitude in them and us. When children feel appreciated, they develop a positive association with the idea of work in their minds. Does this mean they will never resist work again? No, sorry. But it is something that will grow if we persevere.

Build Skills and Habits

Basic skills are the building blocks of habits, which in turn contribute to a productive work life as an adult. Skills are learned over time and with repetition. The younger we start, the sooner the habits are established. A basic skill is "pick up after yourself." It starts with toys. I firmly believe that if a little child can dump magnetic blocks out and strew them across the entire room, that same child can be taught to put the blocks back in the bucket. Make it fun, sing a song, do it together, and praise them when it's done. If they resist, stay positive, but don't give up. Say, "Snack time when the blocks are picked up!" It's easier to train the will of a one-year-old than a fourteen-year-old.

Give them a part in keeping their room tidy. If they can walk, they can put their dirty clothes in the hamper—make it a habit. Make the bed together—teach as you go. Share the joy of a job well done: "Your room looks great!" During the coronavirus, when everybody had to stay home and homeschool, our niece had a chart. Her children had to show up for breakfast dressed with their faces washed and hair combed, beds made, and rooms tidy in order to get a point on their chart. After a certain number of consecutive points, they found a prize under their pillow.

Some friends in Maine live in a house with a modest entryway. The kids were required to take their shoes and coats down to the basement when entering the house. If they left their shoes in the hallway as a trip hazard for others, they had to take the shoes down ten times in a row. On the second transgression, it was fifty trips. Because Mom enforced the rule consistently, the kids learned quickly to make this a habit. I look back and wish I had been more consistent in this area. I should have greeted the kids at the door when they came home from school, and stood as a friendly sergeant, only letting them into the rest of the house when their stuff was properly stashed. Consistency up front saves the kids from just mindlessly dumping their bags, coats, and boots in the mudroom, and keeps Mom from exasperation. Focused attention to building habits offers welcomed paybacks in the short and long run. Everyday tasks must be done automatically.

Some parents focus on building one habit at a time, like for a whole week, until it is well-established. Others do it in the course of every-day living.

Dinnertime is a great opportunity to teach our children habits. It takes more time and effort initially, but it soon saves both, once habits are established. Helping prepare the food is fun, and it serves the whole family. Include your children in choosing meals. Eating is fun and a reward in itself. And of course, Mom shouldn't be left with the cleanup afterward. When the whole family gets right on it, the job is done in ten to fifteen minutes. If my brother- and sister-in-law could do it with thirteen kids, anyone can do it. They attacked the work, and it was quickly done. No whining or delaying—just get the job done.

Build Confidence and Independence

When one of our granddaughters was three and playing outside with her family, she had to go to the bathroom, so they said, "Go ahead, and come back out." It took a while, but she finally showed up again. It wasn't until later that they realized she hadn't quite made it. So she had put her wet clothes in the laundry room, went upstairs to her room, and chose a bathing-suit bottom instead of underpants along with a clean pair of jeans. She couldn't reach the sock drawer, so she skipped that part. She never said a word when she rejoined the family. Her mom only noticed when she saw her barefoot in fifty-degree weather, because the shoes were chafing her feet. This little one is quite independent. I admire our daughter-in-law for encouraging and channeling that independence, for establishing the "put your dirty clothes in the laundry room" habit, and for giving her the freedom to choose her own outfit of the day (on days they don't have to go away). Obviously, she had the confidence as well.

Most kids are born with a streak of independence, some stronger than others. It shows up when they try to feed themselves, getting more food on their face than in their mouth, or when they try to dress themselves, saying, "Me do." Sometimes we don't want the mess or don't have time to wait. But I say let's invest the time and nurture this desire for independence. If we stifle it, they might soon conclude it's easier to let Mom and Dad do the work and end up refusing to do some of these self-care tasks. Of course, it won't be up to snuff from the beginning. But practice makes perfect. How else will they learn but by doing? Praise them for taking the initiative, and guide them along the way.

I recommend getting the basic skills of daily living down pat by the early teen years. Aside from the tasks already mentioned, children can take part in time management, housecleaning and organization, meal management, holding and caring for an infant, yard work and gardening, pet care, basic banking and budgeting, basic home and car maintenance, and praying in family worship. Some of these may not be possible for everyone, but involve your kids in the process, in decision-making, and in seeing the consequences. When they have proven themselves in certain areas, let them take over responsibility for themselves. Respect them for their skills, and honor them for hard work.

Why accomplish this by the early teen years? Because children change at that time, some dramatically. Puberty and teen years can be tumultuous times. If kids have the basics of living skills as a foundation, the teen years will go smoother. It's like money in the bank during trying times. But if we are still attempting to train them in the basics during the vicissitudes of raging hormones, we are likely in for some power struggles.

Working their first job as a teen offers many benefits. They must listen to someone else now. If you have brought them through "basic training," their boss will reinforce lessons learned at home. They start at the lowest level, so they learn to perform mundane tasks quickly. They learn perseverance and new skills, including people skills. Some parents decide their children should focus solely on academics and not have a job in high school, but learning these valuable lessons out in the workplace will better prepare those teens for a future career.

Some teenagers develop a default attitude of being suspicious of Mom's and Dad's advice. They put up their defenses and resist: "Don't tell me what to do. I'm not a kid anymore!" We don't like it as a parent, but it's part of their journey to independence. Do they feel we are holding them back? (Moms tend to do this more than Dads, it seems.) When we sense disobedience or defiance, maybe they are saying, "I need to learn this on my own, even if it means making my own mistakes." Maybe we ought to give them space, realizing they are getting older, and instead of giving orders, have discussions instead. We can ask, "What is your idea? How do you think that will play out?"

Hang on for the ride. Pick your battles. Don't quibble over the little stuff. Just focus on the big issues. In most cases, things will get better. Both my husband and I and other friends resisted work at home when we were younger, but when we got our first job, we worked diligently. Why? It was exciting to have our own job, we wanted to prove ourselves, and that paycheck in our pocket felt pretty good. Besides, we really did care what others thought of us. In other words, we were maturing, and our parent-training was beginning to pay off. (A note of consolation: when your son or daughter is about twenty-three years old, you will be wiser, and they will come back to you for advice.)

Finally, confidence and independence increase with experience and encouragement. Having to make their own decisions and live with the consequences, whether they be good or bad, will teach teens much more than Mom and Dad telling them so. Your children will make mistakes, and while we do all we can to protect them from the dangerous ones, some mistakes can actually be beneficial to them. And it may be the only way they will learn—in the school of hard knocks. They can learn how to overcome obstacles. We take a step back—and a step down by praying. We loosen our grip and gradually set them free to be who God wants them to be. Yet we keep holding them tight in our hearts with our love.

Build Identity

Children develop their identity based on what they can do, how they perceive themselves, and how they sense that we parents perceive them. If we nag, they might think, "I can't do anything right." But if we nurture our little children in their work, they will think, "I'm a good worker." Picture them with their toy kitchen and tools. They feel grown up, like Mommy and Daddy. They feel important as they tag along with Dad as he changes the oil in the car, or with Mom as she bakes muffins. If we share our knowledge about our everyday work and speak to them respectfully, they'll realize we are preparing them for adulthood. If we build skills, habits, confidence, and independence, they'll grow up to think, "I can do this. I've got skills and ability in my field." They will see themselves not as a failure but as capable of work. They will be excited to accomplish tasks. They will be eager to learn more. They will have developed self-discipline, self-control, and self-respect. These traits will increase when they are in the habit of working hard every day. This is our goal. We will have successfully completed passing the baton of responsibility to them. Then they will be on their way to identifying the talents God has given them, and with His help, return thanks and use them for His honor and glory and for the benefit of their neighbor.

Chapter 6

Custom Training

A long time ago, at a wedding reception, we were seated with two couples who each had a large family. One family was having trouble with some of their children. Things were going quite well for the other family. The troubled dad said, "I don't know what I'm doing wrong. I'm raising them all the same." The other dad replied, "Maybe that's what you are doing wrong."

Every parent will testify that each child is unique. Our three are extremely different from each other. One focuses on the work at hand, finishes it, and moves on to the next task—a convergent thinker. Another is artistic, creative, and observant of every detail in life—a divergent thinker. And the third is a combination of creative and focused. As we reared them, I was very conscious of being fair to all three, maybe too much so, down to the little details. We do have to strive for fairness. We must be consistent. We hold them all to the same standards of morality. We raise them in the fear and nurture of the Lord. We train them in the skills of life. We make sure they have balanced amounts of nutritious food, exercise, and sleep. But because they are unique, we need to custom train them according to their character and personality. What areas of life call for custom training? We will look at the areas of learning style and work style and discipline.

Learning Style and Work Style

If you could peek through the window of a kindergarten classroom, you might see Leo, Emily, and Charlie wiggling as they listen to their teacher, while Ella, Noah, and Lily sit quietly. But if you asked Ms. Perkins, their teacher, she might tell you that some of the wiggly kids grasp the lesson better than some of the ones who sit still. Some teens study for tests with music reverberating in their headphones; others need complete silence. Some work in the middle of a mess, and some need order around them. Every good teacher will use a variety of methods to reach every student because children learn and work in different ways.

A close friend of mine, an expert teacher of young children, told me, "At the start of the year, my students and I spend a lot of time getting to know each other so that I understand how to teach them. They need to recognize *why* they need to learn so they can get ready for what the Lord has in store for them. They have to enjoy working so they can learn. If it's hard, we keep on, little by little. They tell me how they think about things. They teach me so I can teach them. The learning builds and builds. If they don't enjoy learning, I teach them in a different way, until I find a way they like. They laugh and say, 'Now I get it!'"

Behavioral scientists have analyzed learning and work styles. They have found seven widely accepted learning styles:

- Visual learners prefer to use pictures; they think in terms of spaces.
- Aural learners understand by sound and music.
- Verbal learners prefer spoken and written words.
- Physical learners prefer hands-on learning.
- Logical learners like to reason things out and think of things in systems.
- Social learners prefer to learn with other people.

- Solitary learners prefer to study by themselves and work alone.[1]

Of the many models of work styles available, I have found the work of Bolton and Bolton to make the most sense:

- Analytical workers are cautious, like organization and structure, prefer to work alone, ask detailed questions, prefer objective work, and desire accuracy.
- Driver workers are independent, competitive, decisive, and are somewhat intolerant of others' feelings and advice. They take action and dislike inaction. They also like control and the freedom to manage self and others, and work quickly and efficiently by themselves.
- Amiable workers are slower at taking action and making decisions and weaker at setting goals and self-direction. They are people-oriented, good listeners, and good at working with others and gaining their support.
- Expressive workers are risk-takers and contagious dreamers. They are spontaneous, non-traditional, involved, innovative, and are quick to jump from one task to another but are not always good at following through.[2]

I might add a few I've observed: rigid routine-ist, dreamer-doer, forever-dreamer, perfectionist who never finishes, direction follower, anti-direction follower, circle worker, risk-lover, safety-lover, rugged individualist, and refuse-to-work period.

The professional researchers divide us into neat categories. They describe preferences or tendencies. Each of us has a predominant

---

1. "Overview of Learning Styles," learning-styles-online.com, accessed December 9, 2020, https://learning-styles-online.com/overview.

2. Robert Bolton and Dorothy Grover Bolton, *People Styles at Work and Beyond—Making Bad Relationships Good and Good Relationships Better*, 2nd ed. (New York: American Management Association, 2009).

learning style and working style, and we do well to work with our children according to their strengths. If your child is a visual learner and is having a hard time understanding the paragraph on mitosis, direct their attention to the diagram or search for a video. If you homeschool, your verbal learner-analytical worker child might prefer to do a research paper on volcanoes, while your physical learner-driver worker child might choose to build and label a model of a volcano.

Still, we don't really fit into little boxes. I believe most of us are a mixture of these types. None of us is stuck in any category simply because "that's just the way I am." We can adapt and learn. We can challenge ourselves to learn from the strong points of others and improve our own weak areas. We are all required to work and be taught in a variety of ways during our everyday lives. So, let's enjoy the challenge and the adventure. After all, variety is the spice of life!

All of us know people who embody different work styles. A friend of mine is highly organized and loves to get things done way ahead of time so she doesn't get stressed out by having it hang over her head. My husband is so busy that he is always working on the next most urgent thing. Our son knows he really gets going when a deadline is staring him in the face, so he waits and uses that last-minute adrenaline to get things done faster. A former student of mine had difficulty spelling in school, but she became the best phlebotomist in the hospital as an adult. Another student found language arts difficult but became a skilled mechanic. Several friends weren't academics, but each went on to start successful businesses. I realized in college that I performed best when I placed myself in situations where a lot was required of me. I'm not a self-starter; I'm more of a people pleaser, so I try to use it for good. Many people find fulfillment in following a job description that someone else wrote. Others prefer to start a business and write the job description for others. Some are leaders, and some are followers. God made us all different. Let's try to ascertain the strong points of our children and teach them in the way that they should go.

Discipline

Some kids are tender; some are tough. A stern look will melt some children into a flood of tears; for others, every type of discipline attempted produces no change of behavior. The better we know the heart of each of our children, the better equipped we are to custom train them. One thing is sure—every child is a sinner. From the wisdom of Proverbs, we know that if we love our children and care for them, we will discipline them (Prov. 13:24). We need to deal with their foolishness (Prov. 22:15). Discipline gives a child wisdom, and his parents rest and delight instead of shame (Prov. 29:15, 17). Discipline will even deliver a child's soul from hell (Prov. 23:14). To reinforce what we have said before, we must never provoke our children to anger with our discipline.[3]

Great wisdom is needed to know how to discipline. We certainly learn to be dependent on God for this challenging task. God gives us the gift of Scripture to teach us and the gift of prayer to pour our hearts out to Him. And then He gives us more gifts when He answers our prayers. A wise, experienced mother shared, "I try to be proactive, to anticipate problems and deal with them before they require discipline. It requires more time and teaching, but it's worth it in the long run." A dad of several teen boys told us, "My boys have a lot of energy, so I keep them busy doing physical work—work on the farm, hunting, and so on. They burn energy, build strength, learn skills, and stay out of trouble."

Much of discipline is incremental and by trial and error. We start out with words of instruction, then ramp it up to words of admonition. If our child doesn't respond responsibly, we up the ante, always remembering what they are capable of. If we are trying to teach a toddler not to touch something breakable, we use patient teaching with stern words. But if our five-year-old is intentionally hurting her sister, we use stronger discipline. Some children respond better to

---

3. Mary Beeke, *The Law of Kindness* (Grand Rapids: Reformation Heritage Books, 2007), 92–93.

time-out or withdrawing privileges, but some need corporal punishment. In chapters 20 to 22, we'll look at positive and negative ways to train our children to work and deal with their resistance. Parenting is not for the fainthearted. We must persevere each day for the short term and be consistent yet creative for the long term.

As we work with each of our children according to their learning and work styles, and as we discipline them as needed so they develop self-discipline, their talents and skills will begin to emerge. Jenny's love for animals and her understanding of biology may lead to a career in veterinary medicine. Henry's love of plants and outdoor adventures might lead to being a ranger in a national park. In chapter 19, we will look at practical ways to channel our children's unique gifts to a productive end and eventually to their life's work.

Chapter 7

Together Time

It's been said of child rearing, "The days are long, but the years are short." So true. I remember the days of endless diaper changes, loads and loads of laundry, meals and messes. (And we only had three children.) It seems like yesterday. My husband says, "You blink a few times, and your newborn is starting kindergarten. You blink a few more times, and he's driving. A few more times, and you're empty nesters with grandchildren." Of course, we all have the same amount of time—about 157,752 hours—to do the work of raising our children. How will we use those hours?

It seems logical. The work needs to be done. You enjoy family time. The children need to learn to work and be responsible. They need to learn to pick up after themselves and help the family. They need to know how to support and run a household. So, of course, it makes perfect sense to work together as a family. What stands in the way? Maybe complaining kids. Maybe our perfectionism. Not enough time. We feel sorry for our kids. We feel guilty if we make them do our work, so we say, "They have all their adult life to work; let them be kids now."

These are not insurmountable obstacles. A change of attitude will accomplish a lot. Working kids are happy kids because they are accomplishing something worthwhile. Have an air of expectation: "Of course you will work. That's what we do." Remember what we discussed before. Start young with simple tasks so they never remember a time that work wasn't a part of their lives. Have age-appropriate expectations. Most importantly, show a positive and cheerful attitude toward work and a consistent example of working yourselves. The following stories of folks I interviewed speak for themselves.

Little Ones

"Our children are four and almost two years old. The little one hasn't quite learned to play by himself or with his sister yet, so he hangs around me a lot. I have him put silverware in the dishwasher, put clothes in and out of the dryer, and place his dirty clothes in the hamper. Right now, we are focusing on building the habit of putting our shoes away when we come inside the house. It would be quicker for me to do housework during naptime, but it's more efficient to do it together because we are combining housework with training. If the children ever ask if they can help, I always say yes, even if they do messy work. Kids love to play 'pretend' work. They are always copying Mom and Dad. Why not let them do real work instead? They love time together—why not do quality *work* time? I praise them and thank them for the work they do."

We Are in This Together

"Our kids range from junior high age to married with kids of their own. We would always do work together, like emptying trash bags around the house and cleaning. They learned we were willing to do menial labor, and they learned to do it themselves. Saturday mornings we all worked together, like yard work and housework. When you do it together, it's fun and you get the work done faster. We tried to not make it pressured or stressful; we just worked hard all together. We'd start fresh in the morning and reward them with play later in the day or do a family outing. For daily work, we kept on top of the mess. With little kids, we would put toys away before a meal or before moving on to another type of play. We would sing a cleanup song or race putting toys in a bucket or take turns if they were a bit unwilling. Making it a fun game is a good motivator."

Looking Back

"We are a farm family, and our children are all grown with children of their own. My husband was a manager at a business, so he worked long hours there. We also ran a farm at home. Later, we started a business, which also required many hours. In between, my husband had side jobs. We were young and couldn't afford to pay others to do the work, so we and our children worked very hard ourselves. We were ambitious and healthy. As we look back, we realize we worked too hard—not because hard work is bad but because we didn't spend enough time talking and teaching them the Word of God. We may have counted on the church and the Christian school too much to fill in that gap. We did have supper and devotions together every day. We were also involved in church and school leadership. By God's grace, our children are walking with the Lord, diligently working, and rearing their children according to Scripture.

"Our children helped on the farm, gathering eggs at four years old, cleaning cages when they were a little older. Our son says he learned to do unpleasant work fast so that he could be done with it, a practice he still implements today. If the children complained, I didn't have time to deal with that; we just needed to get the work done. They felt the responsibility to help at a young age. We had a huge garden. Saturdays we worked together. One of our daughters remembers a time when it was her turn to do chores with Daddy. She was playing with dolls and didn't want to. He said, 'That's fine, I don't want anyone helping me if they don't want to help.' She got up and went along with him. As they reflect on those years now, our children say, 'Yes, we worked hard, but we didn't know any different. We have good memories. We learned diligence and many other things. We are a happy and blessed family.'

"We think the most important things for young families to do today is to give their children a Christian education. We see our own children talking more about spiritual matters, and we are very thankful. We pray hard for our children and grandchildren and keep in close contact with them by getting together and by communicating by text, phone, and email."

I see this couple as being too hard on themselves for not talking with their children more about the Lord. It was in an era when that was not done as much. As they worked together as a family, they exemplified Christian values every day—this was their strength. Values such as devotion to God, honesty, integrity, diligence, service, responsibility, and loyalty were *caught* from their example. Plus, they have made up for it by having many deep conversations with their adult children and their grandchildren and by fervent prayer for the whole family.

Multitasking

"We have four children, ages seven to eighteen. We have a construction company, a hobby farm, a dog-breeding business, and rental properties. We involved our children in chores at a very young age. Saturday mornings we have a special breakfast together, then everyone pitches in with housework; one vacuums, another follows behind, mopping. If they resist, they go to their room until their attitude changes. Then we talk, and they can come out. We give them a puppy when they are around four years old, and they take care of it. We give them a dozen chickens when they are about five, and they are responsible for feeding them and collecting and washing the eggs. We do it together until they learn how, then they take over. In the summer, I have a 'chore bucket.' Each child picks three chores from it. There is one freebie, so one of them only has to do two chores. This is always done in a fun and joking way. We work together, then they go outside and play."

Tidbits

I would add a few more ideas. One technique that worked well for us that I should have used more often was "Tidy Time" or "Ten-Minute Tidy." After supper was cleaned up, we would all spread out through the house and tidy up whatever mess we could find. Sometimes we focused on the common areas, sometimes on the children's own rooms. But it was short and quick, and it made the house look neat in a few minutes' time. It sure made Mama feel happier. (And if Mama ain't happy, ain't nobody happy!) I also used the nautical term "All hands on deck!" for Saturday work or for urgent, spontaneous needs.

An incentive for starting young is future busyness. By the time children are teens, they will have heavier loads of homework, sports, and perhaps a part-time job outside the home. We lightened up on chores and home responsibilities a bit at that time with our children, as our parents did for us. But this makes it even more essential to establish good work habits in their younger childhood ages. If we don't teach them productive habits, they will likely establish counter-productive ones. Remember, what they learn young, they learn best.

The common themes running through the stories in this chapter are these:

- Work done together is more enjoyable.
- Teach the children as you go.
- Start young.
- Establishing good habits is key.
- Being together and accomplishing things is time well spent.
- Working time is good family time.
- Work is part of life.
- Your example is powerful.
- Staying positive takes effort but pays off.
- Children respond to our expectations.

"Train up a child in the way he should go: and when he is old, he will not depart from it" (Prov. 22:6).

Chapter 8

Don't Spare for Their Crying

"Chasten thy son while there is hope, and let not thy soul spare for his crying" (Prov. 19:18). The first part of this verse clearly means we are to nip sin and bad habits in the bud in our children before they are entrenched and while there is still hope for a positive change. We discipline when they are young. The last clause of that verse can be taken two ways. It can be a warning against severe discipline. The NKJV translates it, "And do not set your heart on his destruction." So, we must not destroy our children by over-disciplining. The second interpretation is that we can destroy our children by *not* disciplining them. If we pity them because they are crying and do *not* discipline when they are young and moldable, then their sin and destructive habits can lead to self-destruction or punishment by the magistrates for their crimes, which is far worse. So, it is better for them to cry when they are young than when they are adults. We would do well to heed both meanings and find a wise balance. We have already addressed the first interpretation, provoking our children to anger, so we will focus on the second.

Heading in the Wrong Direction

Children are very perceptive. At a young age they can read us. They hear us tell them to work, but if they sense hesitation or our lack of resolve, they will seize the opportunity and resist. Thankfully, not all children are like this. But some are survivalists—and *survival* to them is to avoid work. They have no mercy on a patient mother. If she shows signs of frustration, they smell victory; she's about to let them get out of work. They can sense disagreement between Mom and Dad about discipline or how much work to require, and they don't mind driving the wedge between them deeper. They will play their parents' words against each other for their own advantage. They may be future lawyers and use circular arguments until Mom and Dad don't even remember what the original issue was. They may play the blame game. If they get in trouble, the first words out of their mouth are "My brother made me do it" or "My teacher is unfair."

They may be pros at making excuses. At home, they say, "My friend borrowed my book and didn't give it back, so I can't do my homework." At school, they tell their teacher, "I have the work done, but I forgot it at home," when they purposely left it there. Some of them don't mind lying; they might even convince themselves they are being truthful. Some will sense tenderness or pity in their mom and pull a long face when asked to work. She lightens their load and increases her own, and they are happy. They may be playing energetically, but if Dad says it's time to weed the garden, their shoulders slump and they can hardly walk, let alone do backbreaking manual labor. They whine, and Dad might not relent totally, but if he can be influenced to require thirty minutes instead of forty-five, it's worth the whining. They might even go so far as crying if they are about to be disciplined for something they know they are guilty of. We parents soften and just give a lecture and a threat of greater punishment for the next infraction. Junior thinks, "Ha, I got away with it." Next time, same thing. Mom and Dad sound strong, but their words are idle threats. When they do follow through with discipline, the child shrieks with pain. This is money in the bank; the next time their parents will be more lenient.

Finally, they may try the vanishing act. They know Mom needs help with supper, but they are tired from learning all day (never mind that Mom is tired too). They know she might not want to expend the effort to call them from their rooms to help. So they conveniently disappear just as she is getting ready to cook. They know that she figures it's less trouble for her to just do it all herself than to go through the hassle of getting reluctant kids to help.

If these things are happening in your home, I'm afraid that your children have you figured out and you are being manipulated to some degree. They do love you. But when it comes time for doing work that they just don't want to do, that love gets put on the back burner. Survival mode kicks in, and they do what it takes to avoid work. They might not be overtly defiant or disobedient, but they are definitely not being obedient either. Or they might be totally defiant and disobedient. They need an attitude adjustment, and they need behavior overhaul.

Turning This Ship Around

If a ship is in a channel and needs to be turned in the opposite direction, the captain can't simply gun the engines, turn the wheel, and spin it around. He must steer the ship out into open waters, swing it around, and come back in. It's a long process. Likewise, if our children are resisting work by crying, whining, and manipulation, and if they are getting away with it, we need to turn this ship around. It will be a long process, but we must. And we can! Let's talk about how.

Recognize the Problem

It starts with our own attitudes. If you recognize any of the above behaviors or see some variation of them in your home, you need to recognize it as a problem. Be convinced things need to change. Talk with your spouse. If you are a single parent, seek wisdom from a godly friend or family member. Pray a lot for wisdom. Mine the Scriptures for advice. Don't be discouraged; part of parenting is assessing and making those midcourse corrections. Even the best parents are constantly adjusting. Remember, our children are sinners, and training them is a years-long process. Sometimes we solve one problem, and then another one crops up. So, you *can* do this, but it will take resolve. Be strong *now* to prevent problems later. Love must be tough sometimes.

Set the Goal

What attitudes and behavior should we strive for in our children? A long time ago we visited a church in northern Michigan where an elder led the Sunday school hour as we sat behind the children. He reviewed a previous lesson and said, "Remember, children, how should we obey our parents? Immediately, completely, and sweetly." That's it in a nutshell. Not reluctant or begrudging obedience. Not delayed obedience. Certainly not disobedience. But our goal is for our children to obey immediately, completely, and sweetly. It's a lofty goal, but God commands it, and He will help us.

Devise a Plan

We need to make a reasonable plan, one that can be implemented. I suggest writing it down because you will want to refer to it when you implement it. List the problem behaviors and the change that needs to happen. Describe the attitudes you require. Should you make big changes or incremental ones? I would say that a big, complete change is needed in the *attitude* department but only incremental changes should be done in the *work* department so the shock isn't so great. Then increase the work as time goes on. If the required change is too dramatic, you might be tempted to abandon it. Anticipate the reaction from the children. Decide on the consequences, both rewards for obedience and discipline for bad attitude and disobedience. The children might well resist if they are in that habit, but remember, *don't spare for their crying*. It's for their long-term benefit, though they will never be convinced of it until later. Here's a thought to motivate you: picture your child in ten or fifteen years doing the same behavior in their job or in their home. No, you don't want to go there, so deal with it now.

Present the Plan

To introduce the plan, have a family meeting if it's a systemic problem. If it's one child, have a private talk. Make sure you have love in your heart. Don't do this when you are angry or frustrated.

Dad might start by saying, "Kids, we love you. Thank you for (something they are doing well). Mom and I have been talking, and we realized a few behaviors are sneaking into our family that are not good for us."

Next, describe the behaviors in a calm, factual manner.

Dad continues, "We apologize for letting it get to this point. But it needs to change. So, we have written up a plan, and we want to share it with you."

Share your plan of expected work and the accompanying attitude, and explain, "We expect you to obey, but if you choose not to, here are the consequences." Then list the consequences for disobedience.

Wrap it up by saying, "We are a family. We love each other, we need each other, and we help each other. Mom and I can't do it all without your help. Do you have any questions?"

Finally, end by praying together.

Implement the Plan

Then, simply carry out the plan. I know it's not *simple*. But this is the crucial part. I can't stress it enough. Your children will test you. If your plan is reasonable, if this is what you agreed on, then implement it. Expect crying. But don't spare for their crying. Don't say, "I'm going to count to three to see if you will obey," or "I'm only going to tell you one more time." Rather, be crystal clear in your directions the first time. Make sure they understand what is expected of them. Do the task together if they need to learn. But at the first infraction, implement the discipline you promised. And the same for the second, third, and fourth time—however many it takes to get obedience immediately, completely, and sweetly. And then affirm them and love them so that the positive takes the place of the negative. Be resolved to stick with the plan for the long haul. Remember,

Rome wasn't built in a day. Discuss the progress with your spouse. Recognize and thank your children for a job well done.

Don't Give Up

I want to encourage you—there's hope. The behaviors described above come from either personal experience or close observation. Many families encounter these challenges. God uses these difficulties to wake us up and draw us to Him for help. If you persevere, things will usually turn out well. If you are not concerned about the negative behaviors of your children, then you won't do anything to change them. But when you *are* concerned, you pray and work hard, and then you can trust that the Lord will bless you. Stay hopeful. Don't spare for their crying. Don't give up.

Chapter 9

Praying and Thinking

Parenting is super rewarding. We witness our children's personalities unfold. We live life together. We receive their affection and love, and we express the same to them. But there are frustrations as well. Most of us will meet with resistance to some degree when we teach our children to work. If we are frustrated or angry inside and let it steam out, we aren't as effective in achieving our goal of instilling a work ethic in them. Our own emotions, though understandable, stand in the way. How do we stay calm when we feel like pulling our hair out?

Talk to God
The old hymn "What a Friend We Have in Jesus" says, "Have we trials and temptations? Is there trouble anywhere? We should never be discouraged. Take it to the Lord in prayer." Whether we need a little help or a lot of help, the first and best place to go is to God. God throws us a life ring in Psalm 50:15, "And call upon me in the day of trouble: I will deliver thee, and thou shalt glorify me." He might answer you now or later, but regardless, talking to Him helps you express what is going on inside. You might be ashamed of your emotions, but He knows what you are thinking and feeling anyway, so pour out your heart to Him.

Reason with Yourself

When a person talks to himself or herself, others seem to think of them as senile or a little odd. But I don't agree. I think we should *all* talk to ourselves! I've been doing it a long time, and I find it especially helpful. Self-talk helps us to clarify our thoughts. It helps us move on to the next thing, work through emotions, and solve problems. Sometimes we even need to reprimand ourselves. Self-talk can be immensely useful in child rearing. Maybe you are one of those who can just think through matters without expressing them verbally, or maybe you need to write things down. Whatever way you work things out is fine. I would like to present several different ways to reason with ourselves to accomplish the goal of teaching our children to work.

Teacher Mode

They did it again; they left a wet towel in a heap in the corner of their bedroom. They know better! It smells musty, and I worry about black mold. My blood pressure starts to rise. "OK, calm down," I tell myself. "Switch to 'teacher mode.'" When our kids were younger and I reasoned with myself successfully, this worked. Having been a teacher, I could switch my mode of thinking, telling myself to deal with the situation reasonably. My thoughts went like this: "I didn't learn the first time around when I was a kid, so they need repetition. Give instruction again, and provide reasonable consequences so that they learn. Be patient but firm. Teach!"

I would try to convey the attitude that I expected them to wisely listen to instruction and reproof, as described in Proverbs, "A wise son heareth his father's instruction.... He that regardeth reproof shall be honoured" (Prov. 13:1, 18). The best thing teacher mode did was help me moderate my tone of voice and control my frustration so I could think through the wisest way to handle the situation. When we control our frustration and irritation, we are not only dealing with the issue at hand but also demonstrating to our children how to calmly handle aggravating situations.

Be a Robot (or Not)

One time when we were on a trip, we passed the street the GPS had told us to turn onto. The voice told us to take the next street. We turned into a mall, and the one-way streets led us farther astray. But Mr. GPS calmly instructed us to make this turn and then the next. Finally, we got back on track. I noted to the family that the GPS never got frustrated with us, even though he had to reroute us a number of times. I thought to myself, *This might be a handy way for us parents to keep our cool—just be like Mr. GPS and keep giving directions in a chill voice until everyone is back on track.*

I mentioned to a friend once that I looked back on the days of child rearing and wished I had been more of a robot. She shouted out, "No! You don't want to be a robot. That is the way I was raised, and it's not good!" What I meant was that I wish I had not capitulated when the kids whined or complained. I wish I had dealt out discipline instead of threatening one more time because I didn't want to see them suffer. I regret that I didn't stay calm and detached like a robot instead of getting involved in solving the problems the kids brought on themselves. My friend had experienced the opposite— rigid expectations, no mercy for shortcomings, and black-and-white consequences for misbehavior. I have thought a lot about this. I guess it's about balance, isn't it? Clear and reasonable expectations coupled with affirmation for obedience and fair discipline for disobedience, mixed with instruction, love, mercy, compassion, and patience.

Visual Pictures

A visual picture might help. It's almost bedtime for the kids. It's been a hard day, and now they are cranky and arguing with each other about nothing. Just picture yourself on a climbing wall. You are on the last stretch. It's steeper than the lower wall. If you lose your cool now, the kids will go to bed feeling sad and bad, and you will lie in bed hours later blanketed with guilt. You tell yourself, "I can climb the last stretch of the wall!" In your mind you anticipate hitting that bell at the top of the wall when you peek in their rooms later and see them sweetly sleeping. Ahh…

If we have been blessed with good, decent parents, we tend to remember the good things they did, even though they may recall their own imperfections. At times, when we are at our wits' end, we might just "step outside" of our current frame of mind and picture ourselves as our mom or dad. We might think, *What would they do in this situation?* It's almost like asking them for advice. And because we know them so well, we know what they would answer. If we can remove ourselves from our intense emotions of anger or disgust or exasperation, we can deal more reasonably with the situation.

For Moms

Ladies, PMS is real—more real for some than for others. You know from experience that the world looks dark and dreary on those days. You know it doesn't take much to set you off. Everybody is irritating you. Yesterday you patiently reminded your son to feed the dog, but today you snarl at him, "Feed the dog *now!*" He looks at you with big eyes, as if to say, "Wow, Mom! What's happening?" May I suggest something? Keep track of your cycle so you know when it's coming (if you are regular). Warn your husband to be extra nice to you. Warn your children if they are old enough to understand. Try to find ways to be nice to yourself during this time—an extra treat of some sort. Exercise. Drink herbal tea. Talk to God. Talk to yourself. Tell yourself the sun will be shining tomorrow, or the next day. If you want to confront a family member, write the issue on a note, and save it for when you feel better, then reassess. It's quite likely the storm will have passed. I mentioned before to go in the bathroom, look in the mirror, and make yourself look more pleasant, even if you must fake it. Hug yourself. Pretend you are your more pleasant self of non-PMS days. Hold your hand over your mouth to prevent yourself from saying words you will regret. Just visualize something that works for you to make it through this hard time. And pray some more.

Conclusion

When we exercise self-control, we are more effective in our parenting and in teaching our children to work. And we are reinforcing what we are teaching; we are demonstrating by our behavior the calmest and the most effective way to problem solve and deal with stressful situations. Most importantly, sandwich each situation in prayer. Pray for wisdom when you begin the day and when you end it. Pray spontaneous prayers in moments of need. And pray with your children in difficult situations after you have instructed them and admonished them. God, our Father in heaven, knows your every need, and He is mighty to help in every situation.

Chapter 10

Monitor Screen Time

Screens are everywhere. Technology is intricately interwoven into our lives. It serves us in amazing ways. Our children need to become adept at using computers if they are to survive in today's work world. But there is also the potential for serious damage to our children's hearts and habits through technology. I would like to answer some questions, based on current research, regarding the effect of technology on developing work habits. I will only scratch the surface, but I invite you to examine the sources in the footnotes for more information.

So, what are the benefits and dangers of computer use? What is a balanced approach to computer use in our homes?

Benefits and Dangers

How did we survive without our cell phones and our laptops in "the old days"? How did we keep track of family without texting, navigate without GPS, and find information without search engines? How did we easily insert new ideas on the first page of our term papers before word processors or collaborate with our coworkers across thousands of miles prior to the cloud?

We depend on technology every day. We stay connected with family and friends, near and far. We hear their voices and see their faces, though mountains and oceans separate us. Special events can easily be shared in real time, even with those who are homebound.

The World Wide Web is accessible at our fingertips. Sam wants to change the oil in his car, and Olivia wants to build a bat house; hundreds of do-it-yourself videos are available to them. Jennifer is working on a research paper, yet she doesn't even have to go to the library—she just searches "pollination of fruit trees" in her browser. If Michael has a special interest in automotive design, he can find inspiration on the internet. What's more, we can travel the world from our living room via documentaries. Inspiring stories of heroism and kindness or nature films unfolding God's amazing creation, from the microscopic nucleus of a cell to telescopic views of the Milky Way, are available for our families on a myriad of streaming services.

These benefits come with a warning, however. Every resource I read, secular or Christian, firmly discouraged media use in children younger than two years. Children develop language, cognitive, sensorimotor, and social-emotional skills by interacting with human beings, not computers. They learn through social interaction with parents in a three-dimensional world much better than from a two-dimensional screen. From three to five years of age, children can benefit in areas of language, math, and social skills if they watch quality educational programs and parents interact with them to reinforce what they learn.[1]

Technical skills learned by children can serve them well in their careers in this digital age. Typing accurately and quickly is a useful tool in many occupations. Children who grow up using smartphones, laptops, and tablets have a natural understanding of the internet. Because of their fluency and navigational skills, kids today have a distinct advantage in the job market over previous generations. Doing group projects while communicating online prepares them for working cooperatively with others in their career.[2] Research has shown that "benefits from use of digital and social media include

---

1. Yolanda Reid Chassiakos et al., "Children and Adolescents and Digital Media," *Pediatrics*, Vol. 138, Issue 5 (November 2016), https://doi.org/10.1542/peds.2016-2593.

2. Mrunal, "Impact of Social Media on Children," FirstCry Parenting, last

early learning, exposure to new ideas and knowledge, increased opportunities for social contact and support, and new opportunities to access health promotion messages and information."[3]

I want to draw attention to video games because they are extremely popular. With limited use, there are possible benefits. The brain is trained to solve problems using logic. Fine motor skills and hand-eye coordination are improved. Math and reading skills are honed. And cognitive functions such as visual processing, memorizing, reasoning, strategizing, and perceiving are strengthened. However, when the content of the game is negative or the child or teen plays too many hours, negative effects emerge. Violent games result in violent and aggressive behavior in real life. Because games are designed to draw the player into the next episode and then the next, many players become addicted. This can result in more issues such as anxiety, insomnia, isolation, and depression. Children are not getting outside to exercise, so obesity is on the rise. Staring at the screen for hours damages their eyesight. And the more hours spent gaming, the more likely the student isn't doing well in school.[4]

Much research has been done on television watching and older forms of media, less on newer ones like digital and social media. Older media was more passive; people simply watched it or listened to it. Newer media is more interactive; we communicate by email, text, and social media; games require responses; we click on links that interest us; we shop; we dream; and we design. Almost every occupation involves digital media. While experts say more research needs to be done on the use of newer digital media, they do take the findings of research on old media and apply them to today.[5] Overall,

updated January 16, 2020, https://parenting.firstcry.com/articles/impact-of-social-media-on-children.

3. Chassiakos et al., "Children and Adolescents and Digital Media."

4. Sheetal DeCaria, "Positive and Negative Effects of Playing Video Games," Pain Assist, accessed December 11, 2020, https://www.epainassist.com/children/positive-and-negative-effects-of-playing-video-games.

5. Chassiakos et al., "Children and Adolescents and Digital Media."

there seems to be far more risks than benefits. In fact, the risks are even greater today because we are spending more hours on media and are far more involved. What dangers do we need to be aware of as we raise our children? Some of these dangers overlap with the ones stated above in relation to video games, but they are worth repeating because they are so serious.

Overuse

"A child's brain triples in volume in the first two years of life," as they absorb the world around them.[6] Executive functions develop, including judgment, decision-making, problem solving, emotional control, and memory.[7] The foundation is laid in the first two years, though it's not complete until twenty-six years of age. This early learning happens "through children exploring the natural environment, interacting with peers and caregivers, and playing in unstructured, creative ways."[8] That is why the American Academy of Pediatrics (AAP) strongly recommends no screen time for children under two years. One exception would be audio-visual communication with others, such as parents and children video chatting with grandparents. The other exception would be occasional educational programs, with parents interacting with them, though the AAP cautions that most programs labeled "educational" are not based on solid research.[9]

---

6. Center on Media and Child Health, "The Internet and the Brain," Boston Children's Hospital, accessed December 11, 2020, http://cmch.tv/wp-content/uploads/2014/08/Issue-Brief-The-Internet-and-the-Brain.pdf.

7. Center on the Developing Child, "What is Executive Function? And How Does It Relate to Child Development?" Harvard University, accessed December 20, 2020, https://developingchild.harvard.edu/resources/what-is-executive-function-and-how-does-it-relate-to-child-development/.

8. Jenny S. Radesky, Jayna Schumacher, and Barry Zuckerman, "Mobile and Interactive Media Use by Young Children: The Good, the Bad, and the Unknown," *Pediatrics*, Vol. 135, Issue 1 (January 2015), www.pediatrics.org/cgi/doi/10.1542/peds.2014-2251.

9. Chassiakos et al., "Children and Adolescents and Digital Media."

The *Journal of the American Medical Association* (*JAMA*) found that three- to five-year-olds who were on their screens more hours than recommended by the AAP showed lower integrity of the white matter of the brain. This part of the brain supports language and literacy skills. Although more study is needed, this seems to show that when preschoolers spend too much time on screen-based media, the language part of their brains is underdeveloped.[10]

Studies show that the average eight- to ten-year-old spends almost eight hours a day on different media, teens spend more than eleven hours a day, and 71 percent of children and teens have a TV in their bedroom. At the same time, two-thirds of parents have no rules or restrictions on media use.[11] The AAP expresses great "concern about media violence, sex in media, substance abuse, music and music videos, obesity and the media, and infant media use."[12] Focus on the Family advocates delaying the age of smartphone ownership (45 percent of ten- to twelve-year-olds have smartphones) and limiting screen time, especially at meals, family time, and at night.[13] These statistics are frightening. Let's do everything we can to guide our children to use their time wisely, so they learn to work well and glorify God.

10. John S. Hutton et al., "Associations Between Screen-Based Media Use and Brain White Matter Integrity in Preschool-Aged Children," *JAMA Pediatrics*, November 4, 2019, https://jamanetwork.com/journals/jamapediatrics/article-abstract/2754101.

11. Victoria J. Rideout, Ulla G. Foehr, and Donald F. Roberts, *Generation M²: Media in the Lives of 8 to 18-Year-Olds* (Menlo Park, Cal.: Kaiser Family Foundation, 2010), 11, 35, https://files.eric.ed.gov/fulltext/ED527859.pdf.

12. Victor C. Strasburger, and Marjorie J. Hogan, "Children, Adolescents, and the Media," *Pediatrics*, Nov 2013, 132 (5): 958–61, https://pediatrics.aappublications.org/content/132/5/958.

13. Jonathan McKee, "How to Help Your Kids Dodge Digital Distractions," Focus on the Family, May 1, 2019, https://www.focusonthefamily.com/parenting/how-to-help-your-kids-dodge-digital-distractions.

Habits

If children and teens are spending so many hours on media, we certainly have an addiction problem. Addiction is a deeply entrenched harmful habit that rules our lives. Media addiction is similar to substance addiction; it changes the structure of the brain, stimulating cravings in much the same way as alcohol, tobacco, and drugs.[14] Research shows that adolescents addicted to the internet scored lower on IQ tests, though it is unclear if internet use brought down their IQs or if lower-IQ adolescents are prone to addiction.[15] Impulse control is one of the executive functions of the brain, and it continues to develop during the teens and early twenties. This is a vulnerable time of life; therefore, it is extremely important to establish healthy work habits.[16]

While our children are spending hours on the computer or phone, not only are they wasting precious time but other things are left undone. Exercise and outdoor activity are neglected, and more food is eaten, hence the rise in body mass index (BMI). Passively watching their screen takes away initiative and motivation. Instead of becoming industrious, they become lethargic. Families spend less time talking, working, and playing together when each member is on their own device, so we grow apart and can become emotionally detached. Excessive TV viewing (and likely media viewing) in early childhood has been linked to cognitive, language, and social/emotional delays. And there is a direct and clear connection between watching violence and aggressive behavior in children.[17] When young children watch violence, the scenes overflow from make-believe to real life. Violence devalues life. It stands in the way of developing

---

14. "The Internet and the Brain."

15. "The Internet and the Brain."

16. Chassiakos et al., "Children and Adolescents and Digital Media"; and "The Internet and the Brain."

17. The information in this paragraph was gleaned from Chassiakos et al., "Children and Adolescents and Digital Media."

a positive work ethic. It destroys relationships, love, and kindness. Why are we surprised when our children do what they see?

Scars

The studies and statistics would be troubling enough if we knew that everything would be fine in the end. But if it's not good now, it will certainly impact our future! There will be scars. Our children may grow out of some bad habits, but in reality, they will probably drag some into adulthood. It's bad enough if their learning is hindered by media overuse. It's bad enough that their impulse control and decision-making are damaged by too much screen time. It's bad enough that they have a short attention span and need to check their phone whenever they have a free minute. But there are worse dangers. Two stand out.

Cyber-bullying has one-upped playground bullying. The victim can't find refuge at home. The bully follows him or her everywhere day and night—online, on social media, into their very heart. It hurts, and it leaves scars. The pain may hinder their ability to fully function in their work. For some victims, it has driven them to suicide.

In all the hours children and teens spend on their devices, they will certainly be exposed to pornography. They don't even have to search for it; it will find them. Many will survive, but many will have scars. The visual images they are too young to see and that are perverse in nature leave a deep impression on their minds and hearts. Human sexuality is so deeply personal that curiosity draws them in. Many adults who are addicted to porn first saw an illicit picture at a young age. Porn addiction destroys love, lives, and families. It consumes the thoughts to the point of intruding on their daily work.

So here is the irony. Our lives are flooded with media. We depend on it. We need it for our daily work. Yet it's dangerous in so many ways. So where is the balance?

A Balanced Approach

I once heard this analogy. A family invited a man to stay in their home. This guest helped teach and train the children. At first things went well. But then he started to lead them in a direction contrary to the parents' teaching, subtly at first, then more boldly. It took a while for the parents to notice. They didn't like it, but they didn't take any action. Eventually, the children turned against their parents and everything they taught.

You would say, "Throw the scoundrel out! Why would you allow anyone to influence your children against your principles? That's like allowing someone to throw mud on the floor while you are mopping." But isn't this exactly what we are doing when we allow into our homes media that is diametrically opposed to our biblical teaching? Yes, there is plenty of good content that can be accessed through digital media, and much is neutral and factual, but so much of it is *really bad*! It is from Satan—violence, sinful sexual content, lying, promotion of evil, and vilifying what is good. Friends, we must protect our children—especially the little ones in their formative years, but also older children and teens during their vulnerable years. Children are our posterity. They are an investment in humanity. They are God's gift to us! So let's protect them. Let's train them to work productively. Let's invest ourselves in them—our time, our energy, our all—for the few short years in which they are developing.

Technology is a tool. We control tools; tools are not supposed to control us. Let's use this tool only for good—like *really* good, the *only* good—for God's glory. Be intentional when you approach your device, by yourself or with your children. Have a purpose for using it, and don't be distracted from that purpose—of doing work, of finding specific information, of learning a useful skill, or of communicating with friends and family.

When you use an earth auger, you press the point of the drill bit into the ground, grip the auger firmly, turn it on, and dig a hole. If your feet are not squarely planted on the ground yet you hang on to the auger, you begin to spin around with the tool. You would not accomplish your goal of digging a hole. You would fly around in unintended directions, and you might even get hurt. The tool would be controlling you instead of you controlling the tool. This is what we do when we go to our laptop to accomplish work and let the links distract us as we follow one after another. We fly around in every direction, we don't accomplish our goal, and we might even get hurt.

To control digital media in your home is countercultural. You might be labeled overly strict. Your children may inform you, "But my friends can watch that." Be strong; it's the loving thing to do. They can't "unsee" a sinful movie. It's engraved on their minds and hearts. In a culture where anything goes, where people choose their own right and wrong, and where self-control is old-fashioned, you need self-control and self-discipline more than ever. Model it by your own media habits. It's so easy to let your default behavior be to check your phone constantly. I know, I do it myself. We feel drawn to it. We don't want to miss out on anything. The people I know who have healthy media habits catch up on texts and other apps at certain times of the day. They don't allow themselves to waste endless time. They use the tool; the tool doesn't control them.

Intentionally teach your children how to use the tool. Sit with them and teach them as you press the keys. Warn them of the danger. Be aware of evil people who are deliberately trying to snare your children into seeing porn and viewing violence and to even lure them into relationships. Install software that filters out sinful content and allows you as parents to monitor your children's media use. Keep the devices in the open areas of the house where you can see the screen. These are deterrents to prevent your dear children from yielding to temptation and then to deal with it if they do. Even secular organizations like the AAP recommend parents not allow devices in their children's bedrooms.[18] It's very easy to let games and movies babysit

---

18. Jenny Radesky and Dimitri Christakis, "Media and Young Minds," *Pediatrics*, Vol. 138, Issue 5 (November 2016), https://pediatrics.aappublications.org/content /138/5/e20162591.

our children. But let's resist this, even though it takes a lot of energy. Remember, the AAP advises that children under two never be on a device alone, and children three- to five-years-old rarely. Friends of ours reward their ten-year-old son with thirty minutes on the computer after he has finished his work. It motivates him to work and rewards him but limits his screen time.

This isn't all about "don'ts." *Do* use the myriads of good material available. But also nurture growth, creativity, and learning by non-technology means. Form their young minds in a variety of ways. Give little children a big cardboard box, and see what they do—make a little house, roll down the hill in it, or paint a mural on it. When we give them raw materials, we awaken their creativity. You are planting seeds for adult work life. Read stories rather than watch movies; they learn language better, and you have positive interaction together. Play ball instead of watching a game; you will all burn calories and develop coordination instead of sitting and eating popcorn. Have them tag along whenever you work around the house; talk and teach as you go. It will motivate you and them and strengthen your relationship. They will learn by doing. Get the whole family off the couch, and get active with work and with play. Set aside screen-free times, meals and family activity times, to enjoy each other's company.

Conclusion

Words written long before computers were invented will help us monitor screen time: "I will set no wicked thing before mine eyes" (Ps. 101:3) and "Finally, brethren, whatsoever things are true, whatsoever things are honest, whatsoever things are just, whatsoever things are pure, whatsoever things are lovely, whatsoever things are of good report; if there be any virtue, and if there be any praise, think on these things" (Phil. 4:8). Let's pray for wisdom to guide our families to use technology as a tool for our daily work, to prepare our children for their life's work, and to glorify God.

PART 2
Practical Principles

Chapter 11

Good No Matter What

The last ten chapters in part 1, "Parental Principles," were foundational, biblical guidelines for us parents to have firmly entrenched in our minds as we teach our children to work. My goal has been for us to understand the *foundation* of God's gift of work, the *value* of work for us and especially for our children, and *principles* to follow as we train and teach them to work.

Now we turn to part 2, "Practical Principles." These are ideas for carrying out the parental principles. Part 1 was how to think. Part 2 is what to do. Let's put our boots on and get to work with our children. Here is practical advice for our everyday work life—at home and out and about. I'll offer ways to deal with our kids' shenanigans if they try to evade work. Our goal is to bring out the best in them so they experience the joys and rewards of work.

In chapter 2 the foundations of our work life were described as truth, glory to God, love to God and our neighbor, wisdom, and holiness. How do these values play out in everyday work life? By our loving what is good and by our aiming for good and trying to be good and do good, no matter what—not to merit God's favor but to honor His name. A desire for righteousness must drive what we do. Goodness is the great decider—if what we are about to do is good, we do it. If not, we don't.

Good Toward God

"The eyes of the LORD are in every place" (Prov. 15:3) is comforting but admonishing as well. His presence guides our actions. He lives in our hearts. We want our children to experience this. We want to build their conscience, not out of fear but out of genuinely loving God and loving good. The prophet Daniel is a mentor for our children. Taken into captivity to a heathen land as a teen, he followed God's laws in every area of life, even when he had to suffer for it.

The Ten Commandments guide our lives. "Six days shalt thou labour" (Ex. 20:9) requires diligence. We work in the spirit of Ephesians 6:5–9, "as to the Lord." Even when others aren't watching, God is, so we work hard. I didn't really grasp this until I was in my twenties. I regret the time I worked as a stock girl in a warehouse and followed the example of others—to slack except when we saw the boss's feet coming down the steps, upon which we would look busy. It was actually stressful to slack. It would have been easier to obey and do extra work between filling orders, and my conscience would have been at peace. I told our own children, "Follow your dad's example instead; he worked fast and hard and got promotions." Diligence may take years to develop in our children, but persevere and have patience. "He becometh poor that dealeth with a slack hand: but the hand of the diligent maketh rich" (Prov. 10:4).

Just as our children are called to honor us, the fifth commandment requires us to honor all those in authority over us: employers, teachers, police, and civil authorities. Let's act respectfully toward them and speak of them respectfully around the dinner table. By exemplifying Christian character at work and not complaining, even in challenging circumstances, we set an example of Christian behavior. We witness to others by living uprightly and evangelize others in a practical way. Let's "shine as lights in the world," as Paul urges us (Phil. 2:14–16). Our children will sense our attitude and, by God's grace, follow our example by respecting us and their boss one day.

We are joyful when companies like Chick-fil-A and Hobby Lobby are closed on the Lord's Day and still prosper. We take our kids there and tell them why God's favor and blessing rests on those who honor Him in their business. And we encourage them to find employment there when they look for their first job. Whether they find a career in restaurants or retail, we pray they will follow good, God-glorifying business practices.

Integrity shows up everywhere. Do we follow the laws when we go hunting and fishing with our children, even when no one will know the difference? Do we follow building codes when we remodel? Do we pay required taxes, or do we do some transactions under the table? Do we put in an honest day's work or shave a few minutes off? Is our work high quality? When we sell a vehicle in a private sale, do we fully disclose the problems as well as the strong points? When we bargain for a lower price on an item we want to buy, is it because the item is worth less? Or are we pictured in Proverbs 20:14, "It is naught, it is naught, saith the buyer: but when he is gone his way, then he boasteth"? If we walk with integrity, our children observe and learn that honesty in everyday life and in business is the best policy. "He that keepeth the law, happy is he" (Prov. 29:18).

Some of our little ones don't lie and steal. But let's be honest, many of them do. We do them a favor when we catch them swiping candy from the cupboard, and we make them suffer punishment for stealing. When our own children were little and I saw them doing something wrong, I would turn away and sternly call out their name. I wanted to give them the impression that Mommy had eyes in the back of her head, therefore they shouldn't even think about doing something sneaky. I wanted to train their consciences that God is omnipresent. We shape our children morally when we catch them in a lie, and we discipline them firmly and fittingly. Teaching our children to not lie or steal *can* and *must* be done at a young age, otherwise, they will continue sinning unchecked, building bad habits. As they get older, we teach them that slacking or doing poor quality work is another form of stealing—it is stealing time and wages from whomever we are working for. When they express remorse and learn lessons, let's encourage and commend them so the negative behavior is diminished and the positive is reinforced.

Let's aim for good habits at a young age. Why let bad habits develop? They will be harder to change later, if they change at all. With patience and God's strength, let's run the marathon of training our children to do good work. Let's love what is good so they do too. Let's demonstrate the deep satisfaction that comes with doing good toward God. When it's good according to God's standards, we will be blessed. And the good will overflow in service to others.

Good to Others

At a wedding we recently attended, the groom's brother, before proposing the toast, teased the groom, Aaron, for his youthful quirks. Then he said, "The other day, I was driving down the road and noticed someone with car trouble on the shoulder. I pulled over to see if I could help. But Aaron was already there. You know, he carries tools, jumper cables, and a tow strap in his truck, just in case he finds an opportunity to help someone. That's the kind of guy Aaron is. He gets a lot of joy out of that."

Dear parents, let's teach our children the joy of doing good to others! They will be richer for it. To deprive them of this joy is to impoverish them! Some children are naturally inclined to do good to others; the rest must be taught. Educate them in empathy. Point out the pain of a neighbor who is ill, and make a meal together with your children. Then deliver it together with a card and artwork from each child, and witness the gratitude. Your neighbor will be touched, and so will your children.

When my husband was sixteen, his nineteen-year-old brother said to him one day, "I figured out what life is all about, and I can say it in one word: *service*." Joel said, "Wow! That's cool!" But fifty years later, he has a much deeper understanding of how true this is. If we love God above all and our neighbor as ourselves, then our whole life is about service, at home and at work. Let's steer our children toward careers of service so they can not only earn a living but also experience the deep satisfaction of helping others. My sister is a nurse, and the highlight of her day at work is when she can calm a patient's anxieties. A teacher friend told me, "I am entrusted with the task of helping build the foundations of my students' lives so that, many years from now, they can fulfill their God-given callings." My husband and other pastors have the greatest profession of service—to bring the gospel to lost souls.

One of our granddaughters, upon starting preschool, said, "When I grow up, I want to be a hero!" Most of us, young and old, dream of being heroes of some sort. We can nurture our children's dreams by telling them hero stories: a firefighter who rescues people from blazing buildings, a police officer who coaxes a suicidal person away from the edge of a bridge, a humane society worker who nurses abused animals back to health, a tow-truck driver who pulls a car off the highway and prevents another accident, a soldier who fights to preserve our freedom, a farmer who harvests the crop for an ill neighbor, or a doctor who cures sick children. Let's feed our children's appetite for adventure by reading stories and watching wholesome films about heroes who help those in distress. Do not show *any* videos that glorify violence and evil! Whatever you are feeding into your child's mind, make sure the bad guy loses and the good guy wins.

Sometimes it's just little things of our workday life. I clearly remember picking strawberries and rhubarb at Grandpa and Grandma Kamp's house. Grandma wanted to give us the fruit, but Dad wanted to pay for it. It was almost an argument—almost every time. As a little girl, I observed that it is good to pay for the things you receive and to not have an attitude of entitlement. And I learned it is good to be generous.

As I look back on my childhood, I am so thankful for the example my parents set as volunteers in our community. My dad regularly donated blood—fourteen gallons over his lifetime until he had to go on blood thinner and couldn't give anymore. Mom and Dad served our church and Christian school in any way possible: school board, consistory, Esther Guild, and PTA. Their volunteer work continues at ages eighty-eight and eighty-six years as they work at our church's mission. They even served strangers by taking care of the environment. The sign at Tahquamenon Falls was our mantra in nature, "Take nothing but memories and pictures; leave nothing but footprints." Littering was strictly forbidden; in fact, we would pick up other people's litter. Mom would beautify a flowerbed at the doctor's office or a store by pulling weeds as she walked by. My siblings and I do the same thing! We were taught, "Leave a place better than you found it."

Why is the Golden Rule golden? An internet search couldn't tell me. But I propose three reasons. We all appreciate those who practice the Golden Rule in how they treat us—it feels golden. But more so, it is what Jesus did. Divine yet humble Jesus went about doing good to sinners. Let's follow His example! This leads to the third reason. When we and our children practice the Golden Rule toward others, *we* are incredibly blessed. We have a golden life! Let's be ready to always help others, at home, at work, as a volunteer, or as a hobby. Let's talk with our children about the exhilaration it gives us. Let's "rejoice with them that do rejoice, and weep with them that weep" (Rom. 12:15). And let's follow Matthew 25:31–46: feeding the hungry, giving a drink to the thirsty, giving clothes to the naked, visiting the sick and imprisoned, and showing hospitality to strangers, because when we do these things, Jesus encourages us, "Inasmuch as ye have done it unto one of the least of these my brethren, ye have done it unto me."

Your Good Name

Ben's dad told me he loves to work, so I hired him to help me around the yard. He did a good job, so I mentioned it to my mom. She hired him to transplant some myrtle. We stopped to get strawberries at a local farm and found out Ben works there. His employer even told me, "He sharpens the tools and does a bunch of other things. He's a great worker." Ben is building a good name for himself and getting rewarded by getting more work and gaining experience.

"A good name is rather to be chosen than great riches, and loving favour rather than silver and gold" (Prov. 22:1). Our reputation is important. It starts young and builds. "Even a child is known by his doings, whether his work be pure, and whether it be right" (Prov. 20:11). If we stress to our children that God sees all we do and people see some of what we do, then we hope and pray they grow up understanding the value of being good. A balance is needed. We don't want them to be so focused on establishing themselves that they become selfish and proud. We also don't want them to simply be people pleasers, but the reality is they are building a reputation one way or the other. Integrity and diligence will carry a young person far in the work world—I would say even further than intelligence. From a teacher's point of view, a child with a high IQ who breezed through school but did not learn to work hard is less prepared for the work world than a student of average intelligence who has learned to be industrious.

I can just sense some of you sighing at this moment. You are thinking, "I haven't built the greatest reputation myself," or "My child is heading in the wrong direction, and they don't seem to even care." There is hope! There is redemption! Jesus Christ can turn around the ship of our lives. He can repair our reputation, and our child's, by giving us the will to do good. He can give us perseverance so that eventually our reputation is repaired. He can help us find the rewards and the joy of following goodness in our work—toward God and to others. Let's heed the words of Proverbs 4:23, "Keep thy heart with all diligence; for out of it are the issues of life."

Chapter 12

Work Is What We Do

For naturally diligent children and adults, much of this and the next chapters will be common sense. When you are a "Just do your work" type person, you see what must be done and you do it, simple as that. It would try your patience to read about work; you say, "Just let me get to work!"

The rest of us, though, sometimes need to consciously think through our work. Our children may need advice on how to approach a task. They might need a little motivation (or a lot!). It's ideal if they can muster up that motivation from within. But if not, we parents will have to exert outside pressure. If given a choice, some of our children would rather avoid work altogether. But work is what we do. It's the stuff of life. So let's get on with it.

No Wiggle Room

A child doesn't have to be very old to sense when play changes to work. And some don't like it. A toddler can strew her doll and doll clothes over the playroom floor with zeal, but when Mommy says, "It's time to tidy up," suddenly she feels paralyzed. I've seen it with my kids and my grandkids. I try to stay pleasant while still insisting the work get done. I tell them, "When we are finished, we will have lunch." Or I say, "We'll do this together. I pick up a toy, then it's your turn." Make it fun as you train them. For the really little ones, I take their hand, make them pick up a toy, and cheer when they do it. I keep it positive. But if they are capable of the task and they choose the negative, so be it. I cheerfully say, "You know how to put your toys away. When you are finished, you can join us for lunch." And then don't allow them to wander away or do anything else until the job is done. Certainly, do not give one bite of food until they have finished the job. They may have even earned discipline if their attitude was poor.

Some children resist work in their minds and hearts. That was me. I knew I couldn't disobey; my parents wouldn't tolerate that. But I agonized in my mind over ways to wiggle out of work or do the bare minimum. So, what happened? Procrastination. While I was grappling with the inevitability of work, my brother and sisters just got busy and did their part. By the time they were finished, I was still moaning and groaning. And the work still had to be done. So, finally, I did it, but how much easier if I had just accepted the circumstances and done it right away.

Let's take our children to "ant school." Watch those creatures scurry around the ant hill. Study their habits. Then read Proverbs 6:6–8 and "consider her ways, and be wise: which having no guide, overseer, or ruler, provideth her meat in the summer, and gathereth her food in the harvest."

We can help our children think through the mental process of how to approach a task. If they are old enough to tell us what they are thinking, we can reason with them. Say to your child, "You're telling me that you don't like to clean your room because you don't know where to start. What is the easiest part to start with?"

"Putting my clothes away. Then making my bed."

"Okay, that's a great start. Once you do those, you'll see your way through to the rest."

Give encouragement and instruction.

If they resist and refuse to receive help with reasoning their way through a task, and if they know what they have to do and are capable of it, then the "natural consequences" (chapter 20) kick in. Find something they enjoy and remove it from them—time with friends, play or recreation, their phone—until the job is done, but longer if they throw a fit. And don't spare for their crying. Stay calm, and don't feel guilty. You were positive and pleasant until they chose to make it negative.

There's no comparison between the joy of accomplishment and the guilt of avoidance. If our children don't seek out this joy for themselves, we need to force the experience on them until they do. They need to taste the dignity that comes with working, whether they like the work or not.

The older child who has an aversion for work gets more creative in trying to avoid labor pains. If they detect a sliver of capitulation in your tone, they will capitalize on your weakness in order to get out of work. If they think you will forget, they are happy to wait it out. If they sneakily do a half job and get away with it, they count it a victory. A teen may argue. Some may lie. If defiance was not squelched in their younger years, it will probably show itself again when their hormones are changing them from a child to an adult.

But the bottom line is this: the work must get done. Consistency is the key. No wiggle room. No empty threats. No negotiation once you have given the assignment. You must follow up on their behavior. Tough love may be necessary. They must know there *will be* repercussions if they neglect their duty. If they choose the pain pathway, arrange the circumstances so that the consequences of *not* doing the work are more painful than the work itself. Then they will work. When they do, the positive consequences must be pleasant enough for them to obey quicker the next time.

Once the reality sets in that work is a big part of life, and they accept it, they will be more content. When they give up the battle and realize it's more trouble to avoid work than to do the work, they will acquiesce. Parents, persevere! Be prayerful, wise, strong, and decisive, and trust in God for the long haul.

Mundane Work

Every job has its boring parts. Even the most talented pianist must practice scales. A highly skilled doctor had to study many late nights to achieve his position and still has to keep abreast of the newest research. A lawyer needs to delve into the details of each case. We mothers have the reward of witnessing milestones in our children's lives, but we must change a lot of diapers and wash many loads of laundry to get there. Dads rejoice when the oldest child can take over mowing the grass, but it took no little training to get to that point. No matter how much we love our job, we still have to slog through the drudgery. That's life.

Each child has to learn this. Ted's first job was at a grocery store. He wasn't too happy with his assignment to clean toilets. He wanted to be a cashier and handle the money. He stuck with the job, though he adjusted his expectations and worked his way up through menial labor. "He that is faithful in that which is least is faithful also in much" (Luke 16:10). It's an exercise in humility to do common work.

We need to intentionally have our children do repetitive work. They need to develop mental stamina, patience, and perseverance to stick with a job until it's finished. They need to develop proficiency in everyday tasks. If our children whine and complain, we stay calm, but we show absolutely no pity. They need to count their blessings that they are capable of work and just get busy. If they keep complaining, they need to do *more* of the same boring work until they realize that whining is not a winning option. If we give in to their whining, we are rewarding it.

We can assist our children by setting an example and by sharing how we deal with boring work. "Get it done first. Think about something else while you're working. Listen to something worthwhile as you work. Enjoy it when it's done." During strawberry season, my mom would get us four kids up early on a designated morning, feed us breakfast, and then it was off to the U-pick strawberry field. A couple hours and many quarts later, we arrived home. Strawberries with sugar on toast was our reward. This was followed by hours more of hulling the berries and making jam, which took most of the day, but the boring repetition was offset by the fun of working together and tasty eating. We have fond memories of those times.

Benefits come when we accept the mundane parts of work. I once heard a quote, "It's good to do something unpleasant every day"—for fortitude, I suppose. A friend replied, "I do. I get out of bed." Yes, it starts there. Let's do our children a favor and develop their self-discipline at home by requiring them to do tasks they don't like or are boring or repetitive so they don't have a rude awakening when they enter the work world. We will do their future boss a favor when they can stick with a lowly job for hours. They will also experience the side effects of joy and dignity and the satisfaction of a job well done.

Work Before Play

Susie's mom laid out the plan for some gardening after lunch. Susie said, "Let's first have a cup of tea and look at some Magnolia books." It sounded enjoyable to Mom, but she stuck with her plan. "We will do the work first, then when we're hot and thirsty, we'll have iced tea and cookies and look at those books." For some kids, the very *thought* of work is so exhausting. They feel like they need a break before they even start. But it's not a break if you didn't work. We don't need an appetizer to our work; we just need to get started working! The break is an earned reward. As Elisabeth Elliot states, "Work is a blessing. God has so arranged the world that work is necessary, and He gives us hands and strength to do it. The enjoyment of leisure would be nothing if we only had leisure. It is the joy of work well done that enables us to enjoy rest, just as it is the experiences of hunger and thirst that make food and drink such pleasures."[1]

Play is an incentive. When the Engelsma kids got home from school, there was always work on the fruit farm to do. After a snack

---

1. Elisabeth Elliot, *Joyful Surrender: 7 Disciplines for the Believer's Life* (Grand Rapids: Revell, 1982), 125.

and a little sit-down and a chat about the day, it was off to the barn or the orchard to do the assigned tasks. When the work was done, they could play. So it was up to each child whether it took one hour or two. Working well and working fast paid off in the form of more playtime.

That's the way our world is set up. Work is what we do. We are rewarded by a paycheck and rest. It's a good way to live. It's a God-ordained plan. It gives us purpose and value. Just ask someone who can't work. As I write this, we are in the COVID-19 pandemic. My husband and I contracted the virus; I had a mild case, and his was more severe. Joel normally works about eighty hours a week, but he could only sleep, eat, and go for slow walks. He couldn't think, work, or even pray. He was miserable. Thankfully, it only lasted two weeks. He looks back on it and calls the first, hardest week "the dark night of my soul." We were created to work. Work is a huge blessing! Let's prepare our children for adult life so they can experience the fulfillment and joy of work, for "the sleep of a labouring man is sweet" (Eccl. 5:12).

Chapter 13

Let's Go

Some children are in high gear from dawn to dusk, so their parents must steer their energy in a productive direction. Other children seem to have their parking brake on all the time, therefore their moms and dads need to find ways to accelerate them. Most children have an attraction to certain types of work and an aversion to others. Each child is unique. But no matter what their personality is, every child needs to learn to work at both desirable and undesirable tasks. Kids have tendencies that carry over into adulthood, yet character traits are not set in cement. We can teach our children ways to shore up their weaknesses while we guide them to capitalize on their strengths. It's an exciting journey discovering their special talents. We need God's help as we train and guide them along the way.

Just Get Started

Admiral William McRaven, a former Navy SEAL and retired commander of the US Special Operations Command, addressed University of Texas graduates in 2014:

> If you want to change the world, start off by making your bed.
> If you make your bed every morning you will have accom-
> plished your first task of the day. It will give you a small sense
> of pride and will encourage you to do another, and another,
> and another. At the end of the day, that one task completed

will turn into many tasks completed. Making your bed will also reinforce the fact that the little things in your life matter. If you can't do the little things right, you'll never be able to do the big things right. And if, by chance, you have a miserable day, you will come home to a bed that is made. That *you* made. And a made bed is an encouragement that tomorrow will be better.[1]

Why has this speech garnered over twelve million views? Admiral McRaven's remarks not only ring true but encourage us. He reminds us that if we just get started, we are in motion. Our minds are engaged. We complete the first task and move on to the next one. We have a sense of accomplishment, though it be small, and then look for more. Admiral McRaven inspires us toward achieving the big things by diligently doing the little things. We do our children a favor when we make sure they experience this.

In physics, Newton's first law of motion is about inertia. Inertia of rest means that an object at rest stays at rest until some force moves upon it; inertia of motion means that a moving object will keep moving until another force acts upon it to stop it; and inertia of direction means that an object will keep moving in the same direction unless a force changes its direction.[2] We can apply this to work. A child at rest may not want to work. But a force (Dad or Mom) makes him start working. Once he is set in motion, things are good—he's got the momentum. He will continue in the right direction, performing his task, until it's finished or something interrupts him.

What are some forces that hinder inertia of work, and how do we overcome these hindrances? Whining is one: "I'm tired." How do you combat whining? Show no pity. Respond with something like, "We just finished our vacation, Drew. You are well rested. We'll unload the camper all together." Children whine because it works.

---

1. Texas Exes, "University of Texas at Austin 2014 Commencement Address—Admiral William H. McRaven," YouTube, May 19, 2014, https://www.youtube.com/watch?v=pxBQLFLei70.

2. Jennifer Betts, "Examples of Inertia," Your Dictionary, accessed December 14, 2020, https://examples.yourdictionary.com/examples-of-inertia.html

But if they learn that they will be "rewarded" with more work, that behavior will soon disappear. Drew will learn to not dwell on "I don't feel like working." He will move on to "I will work." Eventually, he will come to "Work is good."

Distractions also hinder work. For instance, Sally constantly checks her phone, which interrupts her train of thought and decreases her productivity. Whatever the distraction is, it must be removed or minimized. Why not try using the object of distraction as a reward? Without nagging and while staying positive, say, "Sally, your phone is important to you, but it's interrupting your work and making it take longer. We are going to lay it aside, focus on the task, and then you can take a break and check your phone." Delayed gratification is a lesson that children need to learn in order to mature.

As a procrastinator, I could always relate to the saying "A job begun is half done." It wasn't until I wrote this book that I realized I had the saying wrong (see chapter 15 for the correct version). But I stand by my version. We may dread a task, and this causes delay. But if we just get started, we are well on our way. Our thoughts are in gear. One step at a time, just like climbing a mountain. Don't think about how big the job is, just put one foot in front of the other.

Just getting started with work can be like jumping into a chilly lake. It's an uncomfortable shock at first, but if you swim like mad, you will get used to the water in no time—and then you will even find it refreshing. Assure your child that getting into a task can be challenging, but once they get started and work with vigor, they will be energized!

Forward Motion

Once you get started, keep moving. Even slow motion is better than no motion. A speed of one mile per hour times ten hours will carry you ten miles. But zero miles per hour times ten hours will find you right where you started. Of course, moving faster is better, and that will happen as our children develop proficiency with tasks.

Children need to absorb the wisdom of the fable "The Tortoise and the Hare." The hare mocked the tortoise for being slow, so the tortoise challenged him to a race. The hare took off and was so far ahead that he took a nap. The tortoise steadily plodded on, right past the sleeping hare. By the time the hare awoke, the tortoise was near the finish line, and the hare could not catch up, so the tortoise won. The lesson? Steady working gets the job done. Consistency is better than sporadic work.

I chatted with a lady in line in the grocery store once who told me how she was raising her grandson. She wanted to make sure he would be a good worker. "I tell him to wipe the kitchen table. Then I tell him to do it again. I want to teach him to keep busy." I've thought about that conversation many times. I would change it up just a bit. I used to tell our own kids, "We are in a 'What's next?' mode. We have a bunch of little jobs to do, so just keep coming to me for the next task. Don't stop until we are finished." The dad of one diligent family I interviewed told his kids, "If you see your mom working, you shouldn't be relaxing." Another family taught their children, "Look around. If you see something that needs to be done, do it."

In high school shop class, we measured how tight a bolt was with a torque wrench. *Torque* is "a force that tends to rotate or turn things."[3] If we can keep the torque, or the force, on our work, we will put pressure on ourselves to keep on working. In other words, set the example and show your kids how to "Just keep on trucking."

In most families with multiple children, a change seems to happen over the years. Mom and Dad start with idealistic goals and require the older children to work hard. But gradually, they let up on the requirements with the younger kids. The older kids move out, and when they visit, they ask, "Hey, why don't our younger siblings have to work as hard as we did?" The parents are surprised because

---

3. Karim Nice, "How Force, Power, Torque and Energy Work," HowStuffWorks .com, accessed July 22, 2020, https://auto.howstuffworks.com/auto-parts/towing /towing-capacity/information/fpte.htm.

it happened slowly and imperceptibly. I can only say that if we are aware of this tendency, then we can work to prevent it and strive for balance all the way through.

Decide and Do

My personal weaknesses in the area of work are described in this chapter and, especially, in this section. I don't have the parking brake on, but I sometimes spin my wheels. I'm moving, but I'm not doing. It's because of procrastination and indecision. Thus, I know how crucial this is to address in ourselves and in our children. (Impulsiveness is the other extreme, and that can be a problem as well.) So, what is the balance?

Prayer for God's guidance is our first step. He invites us to ask Him for help with the details of life. "In all thy ways acknowledge him, and he shall direct thy paths" (Prov. 3:6). Then whatever work is before us, we talk over the requirements with our children, decide on a course of action, and move forward with the plan, being sure to follow up on the work until it is complete.

It sounds so simple. Why is it not? Because we hesitate. And why do we hesitate? We all have different reasons. We, as well as our children, need to analyze what our own obstacles are and address them. Do we get bogged down in the details? Do we get overwhelmed? Are we lazy? Do we think, "I can't do this," even when we can—and must? Are we too cautious?

We need to figure out what helps our children get the job done. Janelle appreciates discussing a task with her mom and talking about the best approach. Chris needs a firm and clear explanation of his assignment, as well as consequences if he does or does not do the work well. Anderson does best when he knows what's required of him and can work independently. Stories like *The Little Red Hen*,[4]

4. Paul Galdone, *The Little Red Hen* (New York: Clarion Books, 2001).

Mike Mulligan and His Steam Shovel,[5] and Irene Howat's books *Ten Girls Who Made a Difference* and *Ten Boys Who Used Their Talents*[6] inspire our children to work. (See Selected Bibliography for more resources.) Moms and Dads, you know your children better than anyone else (other than God, that is). So, between you and Him, you can figure out the intricacies of their personalities and nurture them on their way to being good workers.

Finish What You Start
The father of a friend of mine wisely required his kids to finish every project they started before going on to the next one. Such great teaching; I wish I had done more of this. It's fantastic when our children have big dreams, when they want to build a treehouse or have a pet or paint a picture. It's great when they exercise their creativity and delve into areas of interest. We certainly want to encourage this. But kids can be impulsive. It's their nature to be excited at the beginning then run out of steam when they become bored because it is taking longer than they expected.

We do them a favor when we count the cost on the front end. "If we get a dog, will you feed him every day, let him out when needed, and take him for walks, even in the winter?" "If you spend your money on art supplies, will you stick to it until you finish it?" If they say yes, they have given their word. If they complain or slack, we hold their feet to the fire. If they want to start on a new project, they must finish the last one first. Picturing the finished product is a good incentive to persevere.

Emily wanted a summer job at a nearby nursery, watering plants. It wasn't as exciting as she anticipated, so she wanted to quit. But her

---

5. Virginia Lee Burton, *Mike Mulligan and His Steam Shovel* (New York: Houghton Mifflin, 1967).

6. Irene Howat, *Ten Girls Who Made a Difference* (Fearn, Ross-shire, U.K.: Christian Focus, 2002); *Ten Boys Who Used Their Talents* (Fearn, Ross-shire, U.K.: Christian Focus, 2006).

mom made her finish out the summer. Emily learned to be true to her commitments. When our children learn this lesson at a young age with smaller commitments, they will carry into adulthood the importance of standing behind their own word. "Let your yea be yea; and your nay, nay" (James 5:12).

In conclusion, with prayer, God's wisdom, and our own example, coupled with encouragement and patience, we can trust that our children will grow up to be motivated workers excited about the task at hand and who can persevere through unpleasant tasks, find their strengths and improve on their weaknesses, take responsibility to do quality work, and be thorough in their labors. It may take years, even decades, to arrive at this point, but your children will come back to thank you for your perseverance and your prayers when they experience the rewards that come with hard work.

Chapter 14

With All Your Might

The other day I stepped into a pizza shop for lunch, the kind of place where they make it in front of you according to your specifications. Every employee was in slow-motion mode; it seemed like they were on sedatives as they chatted about last night's party. I wanted to wind them up and encourage them, "People, you can do better!" Nearby is a chicken restaurant. Only the drive-through is open during the pandemic. The lines are long, but service is fast. The workers bustle about. Management has devised ways to process orders speedily. One restaurant is a place of diligence; the other is not.

"Whatsoever thy hand findeth to do, do it with thy might" (Eccl. 9:10). These words are found in Solomon's summary of the duties and privileges of life: work hard, enjoy the fruit of your labors, obey God, and enjoy your family. Work is God's gift to us. He commands us to work diligently in our calling. We benefit by receiving a paycheck and other blessings such as food, shelter, and provisions.

Our children must grasp the importance of diligence. They need to see the connection between their effort and the rewards. We are surrounded by a culture that emphasizes creature comforts, which our human nature is attracted to. In addition, voices of entitlement are reaching a fever pitch. They boom, "You deserve free food, education, and health care," without mentioning that we must work for these benefits. This is senseless and sinister. We are enticed to want more things—even that we *deserve* many good things—but some-one else will have to pay for them. We are even told those "selfish rich people" need to be more generous. When we teach Proverbs 13:4, "The soul of the sluggard desireth, and hath nothing: but the soul of the diligent shall be made fat," we are swimming upstream; we are deemed cruel if we quote Proverbs 6:6, "Go to the ant, thou sluggard; consider her ways, and be wise." But we *must* be countercultural! Our children's future depends on it.

How do we teach diligence? By setting an example and by teaching our children to work alongside us. Even our motions and mannerisms demonstrate diligence. I remember my mom walking so fast through the aisles of the grocery store that my siblings and I had to run to keep up with her. She moved with purpose all day long. We can model diligence by teaching our children tasks, like scrub-bing the tub or dusting the furniture. When they grasp it, we step up the pace. Teach them to "master the motion, then just move faster." Get excited about increasing productivity! Let's challenge ourselves to get more done.

Train your kids to zoom in on a task. When they wander off, rein them in until the job is finished. Explain that blinders on a horse keep the horse focused on the goal. Tell them, "Be like that horse." Rein-force industriousness, especially when you see it in a nonindustrious child. Affirm them when they take initiative and are successful. Tell them about Erin, who was hired for a physical job because of her bone-crushing handshake and industrious demeanor, even though the guy she was competing against was much bigger.

Explain that time goes faster when you work, compared to just thinking about how you don't want to work. Then require them to work hard to prove it. Parkinson's Law says, "Work expands to fill the time available for its completion."[1] Show them they can spend either

---

1. A proverb coined by C. Northcote Parkinson, Dictionary.com, accessed Jan-uary 8, 2021, https://www.dictionary.com/browse/work-expands-to-fill-the-time-available-for-its-completion.

five minutes or five hours unloading the dishwasher. The difference is diligence—they choose. Point out how absolutely boring laziness is. If they won't listen to reason, use action and consequences, like the removal of privileges.

Teach them that their attitude toward a task makes a difference. Mind over matter. If they are confident that they can do the task and they intend to persevere even if they meet obstacles, they will likely succeed. My husband and the Reformation Heritage Books staff took on reprinting the works of William Perkins. It had never been done before because it was so big. But after years of work, the project was completed. Encourage your children, "You can do this job. Approach it with energy. Give it your best."

It may take us years to teach our children to be consistently diligent, but when they learn it, they will have a tool in their toolbox that can be applied to any situation in life—in their full-time occupations or their domestic or community lives.

Diligence not only brings benefits into our own lives and the lives of our children but it also benefits others. And diligence glorifies God. Let's look at these three aspects of working with all our might.

For Our Own Benefit

Make your children work for their stuff, starting at a young age. Explain the concept. God requires us to work, and that's a good thing. Work earns wages. Hard work earns even more wages and other benefits. Don't deprive your children of the blessing of using their abilities to work to earn their keep. I believe that very young children have a natural excitement for working for wages. They feel grown-up, and it gives them a sense of accomplishment that we do well to nurture. They build skills and self-confidence, which equips them for the future. We stifle this excitement when we shower them with unearned possessions and benefits.

Working with all our might builds valuable traits of perseverance and endurance. Our Reformation Heritage Books bookstore manager told me, "Parents need to train their children so that by the time they enter the work world, by sixteen years or even earlier, they can sustain working an eight-hour shift."

Hard work brings honor to our children. This honor is not for pride, but when we serve with diligence and integrity, it happens naturally. A good reputation is valuable. Isn't it amazing that God allows us to be honored when we are simply using the gifts He gave us in the first place? "Seest thou a man diligent in his business? he shall stand before kings; he shall not stand before mean [common] men" (Prov. 22:29).

In Jesus's parable of the talents, the servants who doubled the amount of money the master entrusted to them were honored: "Well done, thou good and faithful servant: thou hast been faithful over a few things, I will make thee ruler over many things: enter thou into the joy of thy lord" (Matt. 25:21). But the master was angry at the servant who buried his talent in the earth. He took it away from him, gave it to the faithful servant, and cast him into outer darkness. We have a responsibility to God and to others to make diligent use of the talents God gives us.

In the work world, our children will find that benefits accrue to those who work with all their might. They'll earn increased responsibility and promotions. "The hand of the diligent shall bear rule: but the slothful shall be under tribute" (Prov. 12:24). Joseph faithfully and diligently used his abilities, even in difficult circumstances. His supervisors recognized his skills and character traits, and he was promoted to positions of leadership and honor. Show your children how Joseph can be a mentor for them.

For Others' Benefit

Joseph also served others in every situation God placed him in. He kept their well-being in view. In Potiphar's house, he cared for his master's belongings and integrity. In prison, he cared for his fellow prisoners. And as second-in-command over Egypt, he was instrumental in keeping thousands of people from starvation, including his own family.

Rylie's family just welcomed their third child into the world. Rylie said, "Well, now I am a big sister to two kids. I'm sure going to have a lot of work to do!" At four years old, she gets it! She is eagerly anticipating helping her parents take care of her sister and brother. She is invested and feels the responsibility to serve. She is ready to help carry the weight of family duties. She wouldn't be able to express it in those words, but she is living it. And she is way beyond millions of other children and teens who burden themselves by being unwilling to help around the house. Rylie has the immeasurable joy that comes with working hard and serving her family.

For God's Glory
Colossians 3:23, "And whatsoever ye do, do it heartily, as to the Lord, and not unto men," takes diligence to a higher level. This is the most important reason to work heartily: *as to the Lord*. It is for God's honor. We honor God by giving it our all and by obeying His commands. It stems from gratitude. If we know Him and have truly repented and trusted in Jesus Christ, then we know that He gave His life for us on the cross. And we know He gave us everything we have for work: our health, strength, intelligence, and ability. So we want to live heartily to glorify Him. Demonstrate this life to your children, and explain your heart.

My father-in-law read *The Pilgrim's Progress* to my husband and his siblings multiple times as they were growing up. He would read a section, set it down, and explain the meaning of each character and their experience as it related to everyday and spiritual life. In the book, the "muck-raker," who constantly looked down, raking "the straws, the small sticks, and dust on the floor,"[2] didn't notice the figure above him offering him the celestial crown. Teach your children

---

2. John Bunyan, *The Pilgrim's Progress* (Edinburgh: Banner of Truth Trust, 1997), 233–34.

to look up—to not be a muck-raker. Demonstrate to them that work is not drudgery. Set lofty goals before them so they see that wonderful and meaningful benefits are to be enjoyed when we work for the glory of God!

In her book *Joyful Surrender*, Elisabeth Elliot describes Stephen's career. He began by caring for the Greek widows—not a lot of glory in that—but this led to him performing miracles. Then he had an opportunity to preach Christ, which he did movingly. The Jews were livid. It didn't take long for them to stone him to death—a promising life too quickly over. Stephen started by humbly serving and was promoted to the honorable position of a miracle-working preacher. And in the end, this honored martyr was humble enough to give up his life for Christ and still speaks to us today.[3]

Jesus's Example

Jesus gifted us with a life-encompassing example of diligence. His work was to preach the gospel, heal the sick, and save sinners (Luke 4:18–19; 1 Tim. 1:15). His life of diligence was inseparable from His life of service. He never turned anyone away who came to Him believing. He taught and healed all day and sometimes into the night (Mark 1:35–39; John 21:25). Just before He healed the blind man in John 9, He told His disciples, "I must work the works of him that sent me, while it is day: the night cometh, when no man can work" (John 9:4). Jesus would restore the man's sight so "that the works of God should be made manifest in him" (John 9:3). He would glorify God. We must work while it is day, too, because the night is coming when we can't work.

What did Jesus teach us when He washed the disciples' feet? "Know ye what I have done to you? Ye call me Master and Lord: and ye say well; for so I am. If I then, your Lord and Master, have washed your feet; ye also ought to wash one another's feet. For I have given

---

3. Elisabeth Elliot, *Joyful Surrender: 7 Disciplines for the Believer's Life* (Grand Rapids: Revell, 2019), 121–22.

you an example, that ye should do as I have done to you. Verily, verily, I say unto you, The servant is not greater than his lord; neither he that is sent greater than he that sent him. If ye know these things, happy are ye if ye do them" (John 13:12–17).

In conclusion, we can see that benefits abound! We are happy when we serve. We are honored when we serve. "He that is greatest among you, let him be as the younger; and he that is chief, as he that doth serve" (Luke 22:26). Others receive the benefit when we wash their feet—that is, when we serve them. And God is glorified when we follow His example and obey His commands.

Let's teach our children to work with all their might, for the benefit of themselves and others and for the glory of God. No job is too lowly. If *Jesus* can wash dirty feet, then no job is beneath *our* dignity. It means we work hard all the time because God is watching, whether or not anyone else is. It means we do honest, high-quality work, whether it is mundane or meaningful. Providence says this is our work. We work heartily, as to the Lord. Let's pray that our children will experience the deep satisfaction of diligence and service so that it is ingrained into their thoughts and motives. For then they will be on a pathway to a life of blessings.

Chapter 15

Work Smart

"Well begun is half done" is a common-sense proverb that tells us it's wise to plan before we begin to work. *Think* smart in order to *work* smart. If we start out on the right foot, we are more likely to have a successful result. We do the work in our minds before we physically carry out the plan, to weed out problems. For instance, on Memorial Day, the whole family will plant the garden. You've involved the kids in the planning; they each have a section to call their own. You've done research together on which plants grow well next to each other. You've purchased the seeds and a flat of small tomato, cucumber, and pepper plants. You've tilled the garden and mixed in the compost. So, when the day is still cool, you are all out there planting according to the plan.

Jesus instructed us to count the cost in Luke 14:27–30. If you were going to build a tower, wouldn't you sit down first and count the cost to make sure you had enough money to finish it? If not, you would begin to build but then have to quit, and others would mock you. The spiritual application was we must count the cost of being His disciple. We must be willing to bear His cross and follow Him to the end, lest we end in shame. But there are practical lessons to teach our children from this parable as well.

If BJ gets excited to start a dog-breeding business, don't immediately give him money to buy a pair of purebred black labs. Make him present a business plan, work around the house to earn money, build a dog coop, and learn patience. Use the opportunity to teach him about avoiding debt and growing investments. Then expect him to stick to the business when he does it, all the while encouraging him and advising him if necessary. And make the same spiritual application that Jesus made to His disciples.

Keep It Simple

There are more ways to work smart. The teachers in our local Christian school teach an organizational method called "chunking." It can be a memory tool. Instead of having the students memorize a large set of numbers or words, the teachers break it into workable chunks. The third graders might learn Psalm 23, but they learn one verse at a time. It isn't so overwhelming, and the review helps reinforce the previous verses. We chunk when we memorize a phone number in clusters.

Chunking can also be used in approaching tasks. You've asked Alex to shovel the driveway. His regular duties include feeding the dog and bringing the garbage bin to the road. He also has homework, and he wants to work on his model car. So you help him with chunking. You say, "Do the outdoor duties now, the homework after supper, and then reward yourself by working on the car model."

The most efficient workers I know follow a daily and weekly schedule for themselves and for their children. Although some families' lives are more conducive to routines than others, establishing a routine keeps chores manageable. There is no decision to make, no time wasted thinking about it, and no agonizing about not wanting to do it. You just do the regular work. Tuesdays and Fridays are laundry days, so the kids put their dirty clothes in the hamper; Saturday is cleaning day, so everybody helps; every morning they make their bed; and every evening they tidy the house together and their personal space independently. Each family has to work out a plan that fits their lifestyle. Homeschool families incorporate academics with domestic chores. Well-established habits ensure our homes are clean, cozy, and comfortable and that our children grow up capable of taking care of their own dwellings.

Having a clear idea in our minds of what the task before us is can help us approach it with confidence. A child with ADD or ADHD may have a dozen thoughts zinging through her mind when you ask her to simply go get the ice cream from the freezer. A distractible child may stop to check out a spider crawling on the wall, an interesting book, and a piece of candy on the way to just getting his shoes on. And when he gets to the mudroom, he might forget why he is there. It can be exasperating, but we have to persevere with teaching our children to focus and obey. If they are overwhelmed with a task, their thoughts may be muddled. Talk about it so they have a mental picture of how to approach it and what the goal is. Think it through logically. Keep it simple, and build expectations as they are able to understand. Use natural consequences to train them (see chapters 20–22). Don't nag, but show lots of love. Don't give up.

Smooth Operation

The owner of Quick Start Batteries in Grand Rapids is a picture of "smooth operation." Before I have even finished explaining how our car is having trouble starting, he has grabbed his load tester and is heading out the door. It's best if I have already popped the hood so he doesn't have to wait. In less than a minute he will tell me if it's the alternator or the battery, and the cost. If it's the battery and I say, "Go ahead," he grabs his tools and the new battery, I pay, and I'm out the door in less than ten minutes. He knows his work, he moves swiftly but intentionally, and he brings the transaction to a close. Customers trust him and recommend him to others. He's busy and can handle many customers by himself.

Over time, when our children repeat tasks many times, they develop proficiency. Our goal is that they clear the table and do dishes automatically and quickly. They streamline the process. If they don't enjoy doing dishes, why would they want to prolong the task anyway? When they have mastered finishing the mundane duties of life, they can spend more time mastering the work they enjoy more. Teach them to master the motion, then pick up the speed.

Instruct your kids to work on the way and do things automatically so that they don't have to go back to do them. Train them to hang up their coats when they come in and to put something that goes upstairs on the steps so they can take it the next time they go that way. Train them young that, when they undress, they either put the clothes away or put them in the hamper. Educate them in the simple concept of "tidy as you go, so you don't have to do it later." It's all little stuff, but it adds up to saved time.

Be Proactive

Just as we try to be proactive in our parenting so the road ahead is smoother, likewise, we can teach our children to work proactively for the same reason. Take a minute to put things away so you can find them when you need them. Clean up the kitchen as you cook so it's not overwhelming at the end. Fill out a schedule for homework so you pace yourself and don't have to panic at the end of the semester. Mix unpleasant tasks with pleasant ones so you enjoy your work more. Do the worst work first—advice I heard from those I label "super workers." You get energy and motivation from getting the worst job done, then the next worst. Then it's all downhill from there.

In Proverbs 27, verses 23 and 27 describe the proactive farmer: "Be thou diligent to know the state of thy flocks, and look well to thy herds.... And thou shalt have goats' milk enough for thy food, for the food of thy household, and for the maintenance for thy maidens." He knows what is going on with his animals, and he takes care of things before problems are big. He is diligent. He stays ahead of the work. He takes good care of his property and his creatures. He has invested his time and energy. And he is rewarded with food and provisions.

These are just a few sensible ways to work smart. I'm sure you have many more. We can learn from each other. Let's challenge ourselves and our children to continuously improve and enjoy the rewards of accomplishing our work.

Chapter 16

Overcome Obstacles

Let's be real. Plenty of obstacles will present themselves in our children's lives as they learn to work. Obstacles are not enjoyable. But from the outset, let's look at the bright side. God can use challenging times for their good. In fact, if we are believers, this is guaranteed to be true. Remember, "All things work together for good to them that love God, to them who are the called according to his purpose" (Rom. 8:28).

Difficulties can be like pearls: "A natural pearl forms when an irritant works its way into a particular species of oyster, mussel, or clam. As a defense mechanism, the mollusk secretes a fluid to coat the irritant. Layer upon layer of this coating is deposited on the irritant until a lustrous pearl is formed."[1] What starts as trouble may end in beauty.

The life of Joseph is a picture of a natural pearl. He enjoyed the love and favor of his father, but it cost him. His brothers were jealous and sold him into slavery. Potiphar bought him and over time observed his skill and good character. Joseph rose in the ranks to oversee Potiphar's household. Potiphar's wife was attracted to Joseph and flirted with him. When he rebuffed her, she turned the tables on him and accused him of sexual harassment. The same day, he landed

---

1. "How Pearls are Formed," J. Thomas Jewelers, accessed December 15, 2020, https://www.jthomasjewelers.com/pages/how-pearls-are-formed.

in prison. But again, the jail keeper grew to trust Joseph and gave him responsibilities. Fellow prisoners respected him and asked for advice when they had troubling dreams. By God's providence, this led to an opportunity to interpret Pharaoh's dreams. And as abruptly as he had been cast from honor into prison, he was released to a greater honor—vice president of Egypt. In the capacity of head of the department of agriculture, he continued to faithfully use his God-given honorable character and leadership and organizational skills. You know the outcome. His brothers ended up coming for food and even bowing down to him as he had dreamed. When he revealed who he was, their guilt caused them to be terrified. But he answered, "But as for you, ye thought evil against me; but God meant it unto good, to bring to pass, as it is this day, to save much people alive" (Gen. 50:20).

Throughout mysterious providences, Joseph kept trusting God. He continued to obey God, even in a secular culture where no godly person was watching. His integrity and diligence earned him respect and promotions, whether it was as a slave or a prisoner. Joseph must have been discouraged and afraid, but he never wavered. Joseph is an inspiring model for us and for our children.

The Israelites, under the leadership of Nehemiah, were harassed by Sanballat and Tobiah as they rebuilt the walls of Jerusalem. Nehemiah didn't retaliate but prayed that God would deal with them. Then he and his crew just focused on the task at hand, "for the people had a mind to work" (Neh. 4:6). Let's pray that we and our children will overcome obstacles and have "a mind to work."

Roadblocks or Ladders?

While hiking through sheep pastures in Scotland, we approached a fence. We didn't have to wonder long how we would get over it. There was a stile—a ladder with a small platform on the top and a ladder down the other side. We do well to approach obstacles with this mindset. Consider the roadblock, but don't let it block your road. Instead, figure out a way to deal with it. Find a stile to help you get over it, and continue on your way.

Our children need to start at the bottom of the ladder, learning to do menial tasks, serving others, and building skills. We can't let them think this is a waste of their time or beneath their dignity. They need to persevere and build proficiency. Who knows where it will lead to? Jackson mixed cement and carried bricks for his dad. Later he became a mason, then a construction manager. His previous experience was useful in understanding the building process. Be faithful in the small things, and you will receive greater responsibilities and privileges.

School can be difficult for students who are not gifted in language arts or the sciences. They often feel like a failure. Our culture seems to esteem academic intelligence higher than hands-on intelligence. I believe most of our schools are designed along these lines, evidenced by the closing of many home economics and industrial arts programs. The result is that the children and young people who can fix any machine or run a household must wait until they are nearly an adult to get positive feedback on their abilities. If that is our child, we need to go the extra mile to give a variety of experiences and build confidence in their area of intelligence. Thankfully, there are high school tech centers. Homeschooling parents have the advantage of being able to teach the academic foundations but then follow a vocational track earlier if this suits the child. We need to really encourage these kids and guide them as they search for fields that match their skills. Students who know how to work, problem solve, and are honest are worth their weight in gold to any employer.

Sometimes life deals us serious blows. Isabella had leukemia when she was four. She was so inspired by those who cared for her that she later became a nurse. Ryan, a young husband and dad, lost his job when the economy crashed. As was the custom, the manager walked with him as he gathered his belongings and escorted him out the door, anticipating anger or retaliation. But Ryan just thanked him profusely for the privilege of working there the past years and wished him well. Several months later the company rebounded slightly and needed more workers. Whom did they rehire? Ryan, of course, because of his grateful attitude when he had lost his job.

Rob Kenney's dad left his family when Rob was twelve. Rob married and had children. When they were older, he realized that many children shared his experience of having no father to teach them everyday life skills. So he started a YouTube channel called "Dad, how do I?" He gives "dadvice" on how to use tools, unclog a sink, grill burgers, and even how to encourage your kids. He used his difficult childhood to help others. He also urges people to take their burdens to the Lord.[2]

Welcome the Challenge

Nick Vujicic was born without arms or legs. He suffered from depression and discrimination, and he wondered if his life had a purpose. But everything turned around when he became a Christian. He credits God for giving him strength and a passion for life. He began the ministry Life Without Limbs, in which he brings encouragement and the gospel around the world. Nick also developed a program that "empowers students to reach their goals and enrich their lives while serving as positive difference makers in the world" called Attitude Is Altitude.[3]

Our attitude does determine our altitude. We are up, or we are down. We have a choice. When disappointments come, we or our children can slump in the chair and say, "It's all over," or we can allow some time to grieve over a lost opportunity, a disappointment, even

2. Maura Hohman, "'Dad, How Do I' creator shares heartfelt advice on life challenges, big and small," *TODAY*, June 11, 2020, https://www.today.com/parents /dad-how-do-i-creator-rob-kenney-shares-advice-life-t183923. Rob Kenney's You-Tube channel can be found at "Dad, how do I?" https://www.youtube.com/channel /UCNepEAWZH0TBu7dkxIbluDw.

3. "Meet Nick," Life Without Limbs, accessed December 15, 2020, https://www .lifewithoutlimbs.org/about-nick/bio/?gclid=CjwKCAjw34n5BRA9EiwA2u9k3z0f rINNatRd-iY0nPnk6nSlYxW_nOHwTx3iYjTOWmQkZhfXVvLhxxoC5W0QAvD _BwE; Nick Vujicic, "Attitude is Altitude," accessed December 24, 2020, https:// www.baymeadowscharter.org/m/pages/index.jsp?uREC_ID=352240&type=d.

a heartbreak, and pray and ask God to help us through. Then we ask Him what He has in store for us next. We can become excited about a new possibility, and we can welcome a challenge. Our letdowns can be used to lift us up. Better yet, our difficulties can be used to help and encourage others.

In my own life, some of the most painful experiences brought the greatest fulfillment. During a dark time of my life, I had nowhere to go for consolation except to God. That was a crucial turning point in my journey that led to finding Jesus Christ as my Savior. And the difficult circumstances opened the way for great joy later. God works in our lives and in our children's lives in big and small ways. Let's expect good things from Him.

Chloe took flute lessons and dreamed of being first flute in the band. She had natural talent, so she assumed she would get the position. But Janice, who had been practicing many more hours, earned the spot. The tears flowed, and after some wise counsel from Mom and Dad, Chloe realized that she would need to put forth a lot more effort to fulfill her dream. No pain, no gain. By the way, competition can be a useful motivator, but it can be challenging to maintain humility while competing. Doing our best for the glory of God is the goal.

At age fifteen, Michael bought a beat-up pickup truck. It was all he could afford. He aimed to have it road ready by the time he got his license. He slaved over that truck in the pole barn every night. He looked up brakes and body work and carbaretors on YouTube. Every time he fixed one problem, it seemed like another surfaced. He frequently consulted his uncle, who was a mechanic. Finally, the truck started and stayed running. He had the huge satisfaction of accomplishing this task and benefiting from it by having his own transportation.

In his search for a durable filament for the electric light bulb, Thomas Edison tested at least six thousand materials. He said, "I was never myself discouraged, or inclined to be hopeless of success.

I cannot say the same for all my associates. Genius is one percent inspiration and ninety-nine percent perspiration."[4]

Use Your Mistakes

Late on a Friday night, Carter and Dylan were driving around. They checked out a construction site. Some cool tools were just sitting there, and on impulse, they took a drill and an air compressor. The boys didn't realize security cameras were recording, and the next day, police showed up at their door. They were convicted of theft, and they no longer had a clean record. They totally regretted the action, but justice had to be paid. They returned the tools, did community service, and after a number of years, their crime was finally expunged from their record. This humbling experience motivated them to walk with integrity, to work diligently, and to be positive, contributing members of their community.

All kids need to grapple with their mistakes and benefit from them. How do we arrange for this to happen? First and very importantly, they need to admit their wrongdoing—and not just lip service to get out of discipline. We are talking remorse and repentance. That is God's blueprint for forgiveness, and we need to follow it in parenting.

They need to be punished to a degree that is commensurate with their crime. God chastises His children so they learn lessons; we should do the same. While we should neither abuse our children nor provoke them to anger with overly harsh punishment, they *do* need to feel the pain. Kevin Leman offers the example of disciplining a teen for defiance by taking away her cell phone, not for a day but for a week, to teach a lasting lesson. She can't just say, "I'm sorry," and have "Mom and Dad, like trained seals, deliver the goods to [her] like room service would in a hotel." He says, "There's nothing wrong with a kid being miserable for a while when she's done wrong. It's a good life lesson. Parents who are inconsistent in their discipline

---

4. "Edison's Lightbulb," The Franklin Institute, accessed December 15, 2020, https://www.fi.edu/history-resources/edisons-lightbulb.

rob their children of the opportunity to stand on their own two feet and to learn responsibility and accountability—two qualities vital in developing a well-balanced adult life."[5]

Once you have together analyzed what went wrong and handed out the discipline, and they have learned their lesson, then it's time for restoration. How can they improve their situation? How can they prevent the same thing from happening? How can they use their mistakes and sins for good in the future? What outside sources can they consult for wisdom? What wisdom have they gained from this experience?

Always have hope. Discouragement is useful to acknowledge what went wrong. But then they need to pick themselves up and press on with hope. It's all about redemption. God shows mercy to sinners; sinful parents show mercy to sinful kids. With God's blessing, you hope and pray together that years down the road you will look back on these experiences as turning points, as life lessons that worked together for your child's good and for God's glory.

Conclusion

Jesus Christ overcame the greatest obstacle. He made no mistakes. He committed no sin. But many sinned against Him. Yet He paid the price on the cross for sin so that we could be delivered from ours. And that is our greatest hope and comfort. Have you and your children repented and believed on Him, by the power of the Holy Spirit?

---

5. Kevin Leman, *Making Children Mind Without Losing Yours* (Grand Rapids: Revell, 2017), 113.

Chapter 17

Time Is a Treasure

Back in the winter of 2002, my husband traveled to Riga, Latvia, to teach a seminary class. After finishing one evening, he walked from the seminary, crossed an alley, pressed the code to enter the secure hallway, then unlocked his apartment. As he turned to shut the door, he was met with a fist to his face. Within moments his assailants had torn the sheet from his bed into strips, tied his hands behind his back, and blindfolded him face down. They threatened him by slapping his face and poking his back with a knife (but mercifully never stabbing him). They shouted at him in Russian or Latvian. The only word he understood was "Mafia." This was only three years after Latvia had become independent from the USSR. Joel had heard in the preceding days, "If you ever fall into the hands of the Russian Mafia, you're a dead man!" He didn't even pray to live. He just commended me and our three little children into God's care. He was so sad he wouldn't see them grow up. He asked God to take care of our church, seminary, Reformation Heritage Books, and our schools. Then he focused on Jesus. In those moments he felt calm and close to Christ. When he became fearful, his hands and arms became numb. When promise after precious promise from God passed through his mind, the numbness receded and the calm returned. The attackers took everything of value, even peanut butter and bread, though they mercifully left his passport. They gagged him and took his keys and went over and emptied the seminary of its computers. Then they left. Yet he was alive![1]

After this experience of staring death in the face, Joel took a serious accounting of his life, his blessings, his calling, and his time left here on earth. I am a witness of his diligence before that day, and I can tell you he works even harder since then. And his perspective on time changed. He valued it before, but now every second is a treasure to him. He wants to use every moment to work in God's kingdom, to promote the gospel of Jesus Christ in any way possible. He actually works too hard, but he does it because time is short. When I think of people who use their time wisely and fully, my husband is at the top of the list. I try to follow his example, but I have a long way to go. However, we have both tried to instill in our children the principle that time is a treasure.

God's Perspective on Time

What does God think about time? In the first place, He created it. He understands time from our perspective because He created us too. But He is above time. He's not limited by time. "One day is with the Lord as a thousand years, and a thousand years as one day" (2 Peter 3:8). He is the Lord of time.[2] His thoughts are above our thoughts. But God has given us clear guidelines on how He wants us to use our time.

Teach your children that time is God's gift to us. It's worth more than gold. Every living person receives 1,440 minutes every day. We don't know how many days God will give us, though He knows. It's up to us how we use our days. "See then that ye walk circumspectly, not as fools, but as wise, redeeming the time, because the days are evil" (Eph. 5:15–16). To *redeem time* means we are to make the most

---

1. For a full account of this experience see my husband's pastoral letter, "Dr Joel Beeke's experience in Riga Latvia," Banner of Truth, January 25, 2002, https://bbanneroftruth.org/us/resources/articles/2002/dr-joel-beekes-experience-in-riga-latvia.

2. *The Reformation Heritage KJV Study Bible* (Grand Rapids: Reformation Heritage Books, 2014), 1832.

of every moment and opportunity. We are to be cautious and wise, not foolish, in our use of time. How do we discern between wisdom and foolishness? By searching the Scriptures and by prayer. Our example plus family worship are prime means to teach our children godly wisdom.

The most urgent issue we need to address is our own salvation as well as that of our children. We need "to make [our] calling and election sure" (2 Peter 1:10). Since our time on earth is limited, we need to search for God diligently. "To day if ye will hear his voice, harden not your hearts" (Heb. 4:7). When God has worked in our hearts, we will strive to use all our time to His glory.

We are called to be diligent, to work six days a week, and to teach our children to work. But we must keep one eye on eternity with all that we do, as the Puritan Richard Baxter said. So, let's not be materialistic. We need balance. We wisely plan for the future of our family, we support causes that promote the gospel, but we don't love our creature comforts to the point that the glory of God becomes less important. After all, we can't take our possessions with us to heaven. But we can take our children to heaven with us if we, by God's grace, have all been born again. Invest your time and energy in their spiritual welfare first and foremost.

"An idle brain is the devil's workshop," reads the English proverb. If our time is empty and we are natural sinners, then sin fills the gap. Idleness is serious. Once time is gone, we can't get it back. Time is a resource; it is one of those talents in the parable (Matt. 25:14–30). It's a gift from God to be used to do good, to take care of ourselves, and to honor Him. Wasting it is a sin. "He also that is slothful in his work is brother to him that is a great waster" (Prov. 18:9). We need to give an account of how we have used our time (Rom. 14:12).

Does this mean we have to work all the time? Definitely not. Children need to play. They learn about the world around them through play. They build strength and skills. And then they need to relax and rest. Certainly, we parents do too. The idleness that Scripture warns against is laziness. It is doing nothing when we should be working.

We all have guilt in this area, we adults more than our children because we have lived longer. But, be encouraged, God can redeem our sins of wasting time. God can redeem us even though we have not redeemed time. "The wages of sin is death; but the gift of God is eternal life through Jesus Christ our Lord" (Rom. 6:23).

Practical Ideas on Treasuring Time

The story is told that when a new carpenter worked with my grandpa the first day, the young carpenter said, "That Mr. Kamp is sure a slow worker!" But after being on the job a couple weeks, he said, "That Mr. Kamp sure gets a lot done!" I am quite convinced from my observation of workers that the time spent *between* tasks is just as important as the time spent *on* tasks. The inefficient worker stops between tasks to think, to dawdle, or to check their smartphone, while the efficient worker smoothly transitions from one task to the next. Children can learn this "smooth operation" style of working from our example, from "practice makes perfect," and from our expectation and instruction.

My husband manages his time in a simple way. Joel's method is useful for children also. Every day, he assigns his tasks into three categories: 1) must do, 2) should do, and 3) like to do. Then he just starts plodding through them in order. He often doesn't get through number one because other things come up. But each day, he reassesses. He affirms there is a deep satisfaction in fulfilling our duty—even the duties we must and should do but aren't our favorite tasks. By example and teaching, we demonstrate to our children a positive attitude to work, contentment, and the joy of accomplishment. These are all fruits of trying to glorify God in our work.

Joel had a professor at Westminster Seminary, D. Clair Davis, who once wrote on the board, "TGIM." He told the class, "Don't live a TGIF (Thank God it's Friday) mentality—to excitedly anticipate the weekends and groan when we have to go to work on Monday. No, God has given us the gift of work and of time. TGIM! Thank God it's Monday! Let's approach each day eagerly, teaching our children to do the same."

When Jesus saw the blind man in the synagogue on the Sabbath day, He healed him. He explained to His disciples, "I must work the works of him that sent me, while it is day: the night cometh, when no man can work" (John 9:4). Jesus knew His time was limited, and He had to do the work of the Father to the fullest. The opportunity to help was there, so He restored the man's sight immediately. In more contemporary language, Benjamin Franklin said, "Don't put off until tomorrow what you can do today."

Our children need to learn this lesson. Give them assigned duties, with or without deadlines. Teach them not to delay or to think about it too long, to just do the job. Moreover, so many of our daily duties are five-minute jobs, so we need to give our children enough experiences of doing little five-minute jobs that they can see the end from the beginning. Then, instead of groaning about clearing the table or putting their toys away, they will realize, "Oh, that's only a five-minute job. I'll just get it done."

When we teach our children to treasure time, we'll teach them to use little bits of time for good. The world says, "I'm waiting around. I need to kill some time." How about *filling* time instead? I aided a kindergarten teacher once, and during every spare minute, even while waiting for the bus, she would lead the class in singing an alphabet song or something educational. Suggest your children memorize a verse or review the books of the Bible while waiting for church to start. When you are riding down the highway, point out the glory of God in nature. Time is a treasure. Value every moment, and use it to draw close to God.

We can learn from the fifth resolution of Jonathan Edwards, "Resolved, never to lose one moment of time, but improve it the most profitable way I possibly can."[3] In the words of Frances Ridley Havergal's hymn, let us and our children pray,

---

3. Stephen J. Nichols, ed., *Jonathan Edwards' Resolutions* (Phillipsburg, N.J.: P&R, 2001), 17.

Take my life, and let it be
Consecrated, Lord, to Thee:
Take my moments and my days,
Let them flow in ceaseless praise.
Let them flow in ceaseless praise.[4]

---

4. Frances Ridley Havergal, "Take My Life, and Let It Be," 1874.

Chapter 18

Take Care of Your Stuff

Part of the second law of thermodynamics states that "there is a natural tendency of any isolated system to degenerate into a more disordered state."[1] In other words, stuff falls apart. Evidence of this law is everywhere in our homes. Food in the fridge becomes stale. Never does Sammy's room become neat by itself. If we don't take charge of our belongings, they will surely degenerate into chaos!

What's so bad about disorder? Some people are comfortable with clutter. But have you witnessed your daughter in a panic on Sunday morning tearing her already messy room apart, looking for her Sunday school book? Clutter complicates our lives. We waste precious time looking for stuff. We can't enjoy our things when we don't know where they are or have forgotten we own them. Messiness messes with our minds. But when we clear the clutter, we clear our minds as well. We breathe easier. When our belongings are in order, we can find them when we need them. We can use them and enjoy them.

God's Perspective on Possessions

Before we guide our children to be orderly, we need a clear understanding of what God thinks of our possessions. They came from

---

1. Jim Lucas, "What Is the Second Law of Thermodynamics?" Live Science, May 22, 2015, https://www.livescience.com/50941-second-law-thermodynamics.html.

Him in the first place, so are they His or ours? They are His gift, so now they are ours. Yet He wants us to use them according to His guidelines and for His honor.

God is a God of order. After He finished His work of creation, He "saw every thing that he had made, and, behold, it was very good" (Gen. 1:31). The opposite is depicted in the field of the lazy man: "It was all grown over with thorns, and nettles had covered the face thereof, and the stone wall thereof was broken down. Then I saw, and considered it well: I looked upon it, and received instruction. Yet a little sleep, a little slumber, a little folding of the hands to sleep: so shall thy poverty come as one that travelleth; and thy want as an armed man" (Prov. 24:31–34).

Remember, God told us to have dominion over the earth and to subdue it. He commands us to work six days out of seven and to not steal. It's honorable to be diligent and to become rich, and the son who gathers in the summer is wise (Prov. 10:4–5). It is good and fitting for us to enjoy the good of our labor; it's God's gift to us (Eccl. 5:18–20). Always remember the source: "What hast thou that thou didst not receive? now if thou didst receive it, why dost thou glory, as if thou hadst not received it?" (1 Cor. 4:7).

We can mess things up. We see our possessions as our very own and forget God gave them to us. We take the credit and the glory for earning them. We may love the gifts more than the Giver. We can forget to count our blessings. We can complain and covet. We can become bored with our blessings. We can be ungrateful for God's great gifts.

Jesus knows our hearts and warns us: "Lay not up for yourselves treasures upon earth, where moth and rust doth corrupt, and where thieves break through and steal" (Matt. 6:19). Jesus told the rich young man to sell his goods and give the money to the poor (Mark 10:17–27). We are to invest in "a treasure in the heavens that faileth not" (Luke 12:33), "for the love of money is the root of all evil" (1 Tim. 6:10). We are surrounded by a materialistic culture that tunes in to our sinful hearts. We are bombarded by advertisements that subtly tell us and our children we will be happier if we purchase that toy or food or gadget. But Jesus knew us and told us to guard our hearts against coveting, "for a man's life consisteth not in the abundance of the things which he possesseth" (Luke 12:15).

Dear parents, let's prayerfully find a balance as we rear our children. Set an example of moderation with our material goods. Let's work hard but not be workaholics. Let's enjoy our possessions and always acknowledge God who gave them to us. Let's exclaim often to our children, "We are so blessed! Isn't God good?" Let's be content with what we have and resist restlessly wanting more. "But godliness with contentment is great gain. For we brought nothing into this world, and it is certain we can carry nothing out. And having food and raiment let us be therewith content" (1 Tim. 6:6–8). Don't worry; He cares for the sparrow, so how much more will He take care of us (Matt. 6:24–34)? We must be wise stewards of what we have. Let's love God way more than our earthly goods, showing gratitude to God and man and humbly and cheerfully sharing our blessings with others.

Be Sensible about Stuff

How do we teach our children to be sensible about stuff? *Mine!* is a word that develops early in their vocabulary. We don't have to teach our kids to be selfish. But we can channel their desires. Most importantly, don't *feed* their desires. The more things we give them, the more they want, the unhappier they will be. The only way to satisfy "I want…" is to *not* give them everything they want but to teach them to appreciate what they have. There might be tears and tantrums, but that's how they learn contentment.

Each child is unique. Some children are sensible about how many possessions to have. They like their space to be tidy. Others are collectors. They may have a focused interest, like tractors or musical instruments. Or they may be interested in everything. They see it, they like it, and they want it. It may be a toy or a trinket to buy or it may be a leaf or a rock—it's pretty, and they want to save it. I believe we should let our children's personalities be expressed—within reason. We allowed our own children freedom to design and decorate their space in their bedroom. They learned to make decisions. It was a good approach, though upon reflection, I should have required more neatness. We allowed the children one medium plastic bin to save any memorabilia they chose. We preserved artwork by taking pictures of it. The second law of thermodynamics about disorder seems to apply to personalities as well. Most children need to be trained to be tidy. But realize that it takes time, and so we should enjoy their personality differences along the way. If you feel exasperated, try to chill a bit or find some humor in the situation instead.

We have family areas in our homes, and we have personal spaces. Every child should participate in the upkeep of both. It's not fair that Mom must keep up all the shared areas, Dad the garage, and the kids their own bedrooms. No, we all use the community areas, so we all contribute. From the families I spoke with, it seems a good plan is to have a certain time of the week (for many it was Saturday morning) when the whole family participates in cleaning the house and doing yard work. For some families, it may work better to do it piecemeal throughout the week. Having a routine ensures the job gets done more efficiently. Charts help keep track of the chores that need to be done as well as the finished ones. During the learning process, parents should be on the lookout for slacking and poor-quality work. The child should redo the same work until they get it right, and might even be required to do more work. If you notice that one child intentionally moves slower than the rest, which results in their doing less work, then they get the privilege of working longer. Remember, whining and resistance should be met with more work until that behavior is extinguished.

Teach them young to manage their stuff. Clean their room together so that they learn how. To prevent clutter from accumulating, keep on top of things. Donate unneeded items to a thrift shop where others can use them. Minimalism is popular right now. Though it means different things to different people and it might not be for everyone, it has practical principles. We are advised to keep things if they have a purpose or if they make us happy. And the old adage applies: "A place for everything and everything in its place." It's good stewardship. The fewer possessions we have, the less time we have to spend taking care of them. What's not to like about simple, sensible living?

Having a mental picture helps achieve an end result. Show them pictures of hoarders. "Kids, do you want to be like this?"

"No!"

"Then let's go clean your room."

Look at pictures of neat rooms and be inspired. Better yet, make sure they have the weekly experience of making their own room clean and tidy. Then they have a visual to strive for. Neat people often have the habit of tidying up before they go to bed so they wake up to a fresh, uncluttered house in the morning. When that visual is a reality, the whole family can enjoy the peace and beauty of a neat home. Balance is what we strive for. Cleanliness is important, but don't be fastidious. It's not worth the constant stress.

If they know they must clean their room once a week, they might realize it's easier to pick things up right away rather than wait until there is a pile. They will get in the habit of putting things in the proper place immediately.

Finally, here are some miscellaneous tips.

Fewer good, quality toys are better than a bunch of cheap ones that fall apart. The Duplos, Legos, and Little Tykes toys we bought for our little children are now being enjoyed by our grandchildren. And I have Lincoln Logs and Tinker Toys from my grandparents. Some families do "toy rotation." They stash groups of toys away for a few months so that when they haul them out again, they are like new. And it's fewer toys to clean up each day.

Nurture creativity in your children. Instead of spending money on crafts, dollhouses, blocks, and the like, give them the raw materials to build things themselves. Or just see where their imagination takes them. A sheet over the table becomes a tent. Wood scraps become a bird feeder. Mud becomes pottery. They will have more fun than with store-bought toys!

The natural consequences that will be discussed in chapters 20–22 can remind our children to take care of their stuff. If they leave toys out when they were told to put them away, they lose them for a while—long enough to really want them back. If they are careless and destroy something, they need to work to pay for it. If there is an item your child really wants but his birthday is a long way off, give him extra jobs to do to earn it; he will value it more if he worked for it.

Let's teach our children that God gave us everything we have. Let's give them the experience of working for possessions. Then let's be good stewards of the goods God has given us, not wasting anything. "The slothful man roasteth not that which he took in hunting: but the substance of a diligent man is precious" (Prov. 12:27).

Chapter 19

Follow Your Talents

Child rearing is an adventure. Yesterday, our sixth grandchild was born, a son of our son. We have just met him. We don't know him at all, but we love him already. We have no idea what personality traits and talents are hidden inside his nearly ten-pound frame. His parents pray earnestly he will be a child of the King, that he will be healthy and safe, and that he will be a hard worker and be good to his family. His daddy hopes he will grow up to be a mighty hunter so they can roam the woods together. God knows our grandson perfectly because He created him.

"I will praise thee; for I am fearfully and wonderfully made: marvellous are thy works; and that my soul knoweth right well" (Ps. 139:14). David describes every one of us. We are intricately designed. Just as every snowflake is an ice crystal yet each one is unique, likewise, we humans have the same basic structure but each one of us is one of a kind. We are unique on both the outside and the inside.

Talents

As each little newborn grows and we prayerfully teach him or her the fear of God and wisdom and life skills, we watch to see which talents unfold. We eagerly wait for their potential to turn to reality. Usually, they will be particularly interested in what they are good at. They will have a keen interest in the field of knowledge they have an affinity for. Therefore, they will absorb even more knowledge because they understand it and enjoy it. One of God's great blessings is that we usually take joy in what we are good at.

After only a few months in class, Thomas Edison's teacher labeled him "addled" and said he could not be taught in the school. Thomas's mother knew her son was talented and took over his education at home. He spoke of her, saying, "My mother was the making of me. She was so true, so sure of me, and I felt I had someone to live for, someone I must not disappoint."[1] He grew up to be America's greatest inventor, and we all benefit from his multiple inventions today. Like Edison's mother, we can do the same for our children by appreciating and nurturing their talents.

Looking back on the years when our children were young, we remember that they showed an interest in the field they ended up pursuing as adults. Calvin was always buying and selling. As a little boy, he would price all my medical supplies and set up a play store. Later he bought fish, bred them, and sold them. He made and sold cutting boards from scrap wood from our school's woodshop. Today, he flips houses and owns apartments. Esther always loved to organize things; she always had her ducks in a row. She earned a degree in business administration and now works part-time as our church's administrator and is a mom. She helps me and others with decluttering and organizing. When Lydia was about seven years old, she went downstairs to play one day and came up only a few minutes later with a doll outfit she had sewn. Through her teen years, she spent hours looking at formal dresses. Today, along with being a mom, she designs and alters wedding and formal dresses. We have a four-year-old nephew who is fascinated with dinosaurs. He learns about them from videos and can pronounce their names like an adult scientist.

---

1. National Park Service, "Samuel and Nancy Elliot Edison," accessed December 23, 2020, https://www.nps.gov/edis/learn/historyculture/samuel-and-nancy-elliott -edison.htm#:~:text=Thomas%20Edison%20later%20remembered%2C%20 %22My,someone%20I%20must%20not%20disappoint.%22

It will be exciting to see where his passion takes him in the future—perhaps he'll become a paleontologist.

Feed your children's interests. Over dinner, ask them questions about their "area of expertise." Learn from them. Encourage inquisitiveness. Get excited with them. Check out books from the library. Channel their dreams in a positive, productive way. Brainstorm about future possibilities. I can't count the number of Beeke dinner discussions we've had about business ideas. Sometimes we need to infuse a shot of realism into their ideas, but let's do so without throwing a wet blanket on their aspirations. Two of our children would often have an exciting new idea and *urgently* need to go to the store for supplies to make it happen *now*. I'm afraid I got swept in too often when I should have used the opportunity to teach planning and patience. But we learned together, and we had fun adventures, some which led to the careers they have today.

A word of caution is needed here. Run your child's interest through several sieves. Does it have the potential for being productive? Is it possible? Is it good? For example, is your child focused 100 percent on sports? She may be talented, but to where does it lead? To playing on the Lord's Day? To possible injuries? Maybe it would be better to encourage sports as a hobby and steer her in a different direction for a career. Or perhaps your son spends an inordinate amount of time on video games, and you are always trimming him back. He hopes to design them one day, yet many video games show violence or immorality. Could you steer him toward computer science, aiming to use his skills in a more productive way?

Take the long view. Prep for adult life. Give lots of experiences—it's on the pathway of life that we find our skills. Take your kids on field trips. Provide experiences on vacation that are educational, not simply entertaining. Visit a museum or hike a national park rather than spend money to fight crowds at Disneyland. It's much more worthwhile. Check out a variety of educational books from the library. Give them birthday gifts that let them use their hands and minds rather than something to passively watch. Some ideas are Legos, car models, a set of tools, a telescope, art supplies, how-to books, trade books on science or history, chickens, a ukulele, or a journal. You don't have to spend a lot of money to give them experiences. Ask a carpenter for wood scraps; buy a hammer, nails, and a saw at a garage sale; and see what your child can build. Pick up a desk at the side of the road on trash day, and have your child paint it to match their bedroom. When toys break, work together to try to repair them.

Something might grab their interest for a lifetime. You know your own children best—steer them toward their talents. Hone their skills. See beyond their quirks; they will work out. See the potential, even if it is deep down in their personality. The little rascal who is drawn to electrical outlets and tries to take apart your hair dryer may become an electrician. Your toddler who loves to draw on your walls may become an interior designer. Make work part of their identity. Plant early seeds, and be looking for fruits. Find things they are excited about; let them dream. And most importantly, pray *with* them and pray privately for God's guidance on their career path.

Influencers and Inspirers

Our children meet people along the way who will inspire them. Hopefully, we as parents are among the influencers, but thank God, there are others. Right now, our ten-year-old nephew hangs out with two neighbor boys who are homeschooled and who are constantly experimenting with growing fruits, vegetables, and flowers. At this point, at least one of the boys wants to pursue a career in horticulture. Emily had a high school teacher who taught history in a gripping way, her father reinforced her interest by discussing the books they read, and now she hopes to teach history herself. What little child doesn't have dreams of being a firefighter, nurse, police officer, truck driver, carpenter, or president after they have read books or seen videos or met these role models in real life? Let's steer our children toward these positive role models and see what happens.

"In the multitude of counsellors there is safety" (Prov. 11:14). When teens are looking toward adulthood and considering which career to pursue, encourage them to seek the wisdom of experienced experts in the field. Let them ask questions like, "What is a normal day like in this profession?" "What do you find most fulfilling? Most difficult?" "What skills are useful?" "What training is needed?" "Can you offer me advice?"

Pathway of Providence

I see God's providence in my journey to find my life's calling. I just wanted to get married right out of high school, but no opportunities presented themselves. Instead, I worked and traveled. I was tired of school, so I had no desire for college. But I knew one thing: I just wanted to help people. So I signed up for a nursing program. I thought I would have eighteen months to think about it, but after only six months, they called me one day in August and said, "We have one spot left in the program. Your name is next. Let us know by tomorrow if you want it." I saw it as God's providence, so I said yes. Once I was in the program, I did not enjoy it so much, but I didn't want to be a quitter. I was required to observe a classroom for a child psych class, and I found that exciting. But I continued in nursing, graduated, and worked nights on a medical-surgical floor in a hospital. I was miserable. The responsibility frightened me. I went through some difficult personal experiences as well. All this drove me to the Lord, and He carried me through. At that time, I had been teaching Bible stories to five-year-olds at our church's mission. I absolutely loved it. I felt God directing me to teaching. I went back to college for elementary education, and I finally felt I was in my element. While I worked weekends and summers at a psychiatric hospital as a nurse and loved psych nursing, teaching was it for me.

I look back and see everything as providential. My dream of getting married didn't happen until I was twenty-nine, but my dear husband was worth the wait—a thousand times over! In my roles as a pastor's wife and a mother, my nursing experience has been helpful. My education wasn't wasted.

When your teen is trying to figure out what career to follow, suggest they try out a career on a lower level as a volunteer or worker. Job shadow someone, and observe them going through a normal day. If they aspire to be a mechanic, they could work in a shop or fix engines at home. If they feel called to the medical field, encourage them to pursue a job in a related setting. They will find out if they like it, and it will be good experience. If they don't like it, they will be rescued from an unhappy situation, and they still have time to pursue something more suited to their gifts. They didn't try and fail; that foray was not fruitless but was just a stepping-stone to their real calling.

God's providence may surprise us, but He orchestrates it all. For those who want to get married, but that's not God's plan right now, encourage them to trust Him for their future, serve Him while they wait, and be the godly person they want their future spouse to marry. Parents, pray your heart out for your children and with your children every step of the way! God will guide and He will provide. You can trust Him. He gave them their talents and He will help them use them.

Chapter 20

Natural Consequences

Newton's third law is, "For every action there is an equal and opposite reaction." In a certain sense, this law could be applied to work. We work, and there are positive consequences. We work poorly or not at all, and there are negative consequences. This is the way the real world is set up. We have about eighteen years in a protected environment to prepare our children for this reality.

In the physical world, children learn about Newton's third law at a young age. In fact, they are miniature scientists who run experiments during most of their waking hours. Soon after they can grasp objects, they observe them, put them in their mouths to see if they are edible and to check the texture and density, and move things around to see the reaction of their actions. A toddler sights a puddle, and, of course, he runs into it to check the effect of the force of his steps on the displacement of the water. Children also learn that if they start exploring a cupboard holding breakable dishes, their action will result in a reaction from a parent—"No!" and strong arms pulling them back.

Children understand action-reaction and cause-effect long before they can verbalize what is happening. Let's use this understanding to teach them to work. In fact, whether we intentionally teach them to work or not, we are still teaching them *something*. So, would you choose to teach them to work, or would you choose to teach them to *not* work?

I heard a story recently of a mom who has a career, maintains the family home, and with her husband is rearing their teenage children. When she comes home with a big load of groceries and they are relaxing, she does not ask them to help her unload. Neither do they offer their assistance nor help with the cooking later. Something is wrong with this picture. The teens are literally not carrying their load. They enjoy eating the food, but they play no part in the process of getting it to the table. More disturbing, they don't seem to care that their mom is bending over backward to serve them, albeit she has not required it of them. However, it doesn't have to be this way.

We can, we should, and we *must* teach our children to work. Paul instructs us "that if any would not work, neither should he eat" (2 Thess. 3:10). Some of the Thessalonian believers were either idle or being busybodies, not minding their own business, and mooching bread off others. Of course, in other letters he instructs us to help those who are unable to work, so there are exceptions. But for those of us who can work, we must work. This is our goal for our children. How do we get there?

We have already discussed setting a positive example of diligence, conveying an expectation that they will work, giving clear instructions, working with them until they are proficient, and having reasonable and age-appropriate requirements. So then, how do we *respond* to their behavior?

I like to think in terms of *natural consequences*. By this I mean fitting responses, ones connected to the work they do or don't do. Our reaction is related to what they will experience as adults. We can reinforce their behavior by responding in a suitable way that matches their obedience or lack of it. I want to end this book on a positive note, so the next two chapters address the rewards we give our children when they work and the blessings that naturally flow to them. In this chapter, however, we will look at negative natural consequences we arrange for them to experience, should they decide to resist work.

I wish I didn't have to write this chapter. It sure would be nice if we could teach our children to work simply with positive reinforcement. Sadly, this is not the case. We *will* need to react negatively to our children's disobedience, and they *won't* like it. We will need to discipline. Why? Because they are sinners. I chatted with a neighbor once who was a new mom. She said, "I don't want to say no to my child very much at all." I'm not sure how that worked out for her. I do believe we should strive to be positive more than negative, but the negatives are part of the reality of parenting. So how do we handle our children when they resist work?

Let's first acknowledge that it's frustrating—and that's putting it nicely. It can be downright exasperating! We need to acknowledge our emotions and channel them properly, so let's first address emotional dos and don'ts. Then, before we discipline, let's go through a checklist to figure out what is appropriate. Finally, we'll address meting out negative natural consequences.

Emotional Dos and Don'ts

Our emotions are real. But if we lose our cool, we won't accomplish the task at hand—teaching our kids to work. We will only demonstrate uncontrolled emotions, and they will likely follow our example. So, we need to come to grips with our own feelings and then channel them for their benefit. If we are angry, we need to cool down and approach the situation wisely and calmly. It's not okay to discipline in anger. It is okay to explain to our child, "I was very upset when you went to play with the neighbors even though I told you to mow the lawn," and then calmly administer appropriate discipline.

We aren't stoics. Our children may see that we are not happy, but our underlying goal must be their improvement, not venting our frustration or knocking them down. They must always feel our love. And we must always uphold their dignity. We should never express disgust, because that conveys loathing, that we can't stand them because of their behavior. Disgust says we care more about our own inconvenience than about their improvement. Disappointment, on the other hand, conveys sadness, that they let us down, but we still hope for improvement. When the mother of a friend of ours passed away, he reflected on how he had not lived up to his potential in high school. He'd come home with bad grades, and his mom would say, "I know you can do better than this." He sensed her disappointment, but he always knew she believed in him and thought he had greater potential. She had high expectations he later lived up to.

Irritation is another one of those emotions that seems to show itself in our tone of voice. It says, "You are bothering me." Kids think, "I am a bother." Yes, irritation is real in parenting, but we need to rearrange our thinking and words so that our goal is what is best for our kids. Instead of saying with aggravation, "I can't believe you didn't clean the litter box!" as you roll your eyes, we might say matter-of-factly, "You need to clean the litter box before you have a snack." And then stick to your word.

What about guilt trips? They have a bad reputation. Our culture looks negatively on making someone else feel guilty. But what if they *are* guilty? In the context of teaching our children to work, we shouldn't manipulate, insinuate, or make indirect digs at our children to make them feel guilty. Let's not give our child an evil eye at breakfast, while breathing a sigh of disgust and cynically saying, "I was going to *relax* and read a book last night, but then I looked into the playroom and saw a *huge* mess!" It's better to say directly in private, "Mia, I told you to put the toys away last evening, but you didn't obey. Mommy was tired and sad. I will have to take some of those toys away for a while." Being direct and honest and addressing the child privately upholds their dignity while still holding them accountable. Guilt is good for motivating change.

Words that humiliate and demean our child as a person are out of bounds, as is negative name-calling. Our words will ring in their minds for their entire lives. Parents shouldn't do put-downs; let's rise above that. We may see patterns of behavior like laziness, but when we call them lazy, that is how they will see themselves. Yes, kids can be lazy, but they *can change*. Rather than labeling them, it's much better to zero in on the behavior we are trying to change, giving appropriate consequences until they improve.

The final "don't" is nagging. It's counterproductive. We try to be patient and give them one more chance. They know our threats are empty because we haven't carried through in the past. They hear the nagging and realize we are just hoping they will obey so we don't have to enforce the rules. They are willing to put up with the droning of our voice as long as they don't really have to obey. They are irritated with us, but not enough to do their work. Our patience finally gives way, and we blow up in frustration. They are surprised because they thought we would just keep nagging. It is much better to react with natural consequences, which I explain below.

Checklist

We want to be fair when we discipline, and we want to discipline sparingly in order for it to be effective. Therefore, we need to ask ourselves some questions first:

- Have I given clear instructions, and does my child understand them? Modeling the work and working together is great for teaching and checking their understanding. Ask them to explain it back to you and show you.

- Are they working according to their ability?

- Are my expectations reasonable for their age, or am I a perfectionist?

- Are they trying?

- Are they gradually improving?

- If they are disobeying, what is their attitude? It makes a huge difference in how we react. Did they genuinely forget? If so, give them another chance. If forgetting is a habit, we need to do some behavior modification so that they learn to remember. If they are forgetting intentionally or being sneaky about it, they need stiffer discipline for being dishonest. If they disobey and feel bad about it and confess it, they may still need discipline, but it should be lighter. We need to show gospel mercy. Intentional disobedience is serious and cannot be tolerated. We found Ted Tripp's *Shepherding a Child's Heart* very helpful in talking seriously with the disobedient child, praying with them, and administering the discipline.[1] Consider the child's motive so we can train their heart as well as their behavior. Remember, defiance is very serious. Detect it early and deal with it strongly so it does not get out of control.

Negative Natural Consequences

Just as labor requires fitting payment, so refusing to labor demands fitting discipline. What is fitting? Let's look at that first. Then we'll discuss incremental discipline and goals. Next, we'll see how action speaks louder than yelling. And finally, we'll learn why it's vital to let them bear their own consequences.

It Must Be Fitting

A sense of fairness runs within us. Yes, it may be skewed by selfishness. But deep down, we want to be fair, and children sense fairness at a young age. If we are lenient when our children resist work, they will continue to resist because of laziness. If we are too harsh, they may resent us and resist with anger, or they may comply but with hurt, fear, or anger. It takes wisdom and prayer to be fair and find the balance—for each circumstance and for treating all our children fairly in relation to each other.

Fitting discipline must be related to the misdeed. If Sawyer forgets to feed his guinea pig, then he doesn't get to eat his own supper until Piggy gets fed. If Jackson agreed to scrub the garage floor in exchange for the privilege of using the car on Friday night but he "forgot," he doesn't get the car until the job is done, no matter how much he tries to negotiate to do the work on Saturday (because this has happened before).

---

1. Ted Tripp, *Shepherding a Child's Heart* (Wapwallopen, Pa.: Shepherd, 2005).

Our discipline must match the seriousness of the misdeed. If Johnny does a poor job of washing the dishes, just calmly give the dirty dishes back and say, "You missed a spot." But if he throws a fit and splashes water all over the counter because he doesn't want to wash them again, he needs to be pulled aside, admonished, and spanked. If Mary procrastinates with cleaning her room, she simply has to wait longer to play with her friends. But if Mom discovers Mary turned the vacuum on and read a book for a while so it seemed like she was working when she wasn't, she needs a more serious punishment for dishonesty.

Variety of discipline is good. If we were to use the same discipline for every misdeed, it would lose its effectiveness. Let's say we need to rake the leaves, and we require all the children to help. We pay them because it's extra work. But Hans drags his feet and works at half speed, so he receives less pay than the others. Or he could receive the same pay but be required to work longer. When Sarah starts whining when it's time to set the table, extra work might be an option until she learns to obey immediately, completely, and sweetly. If she presents the same behavior another day, she may need to spend some time in her room adjusting her attitude, and then come out and do the work willingly.

Increments

Rome wasn't built in a day. Teaching our children to work takes years. Some children develop slowly at a young age, then we are surprised when things suddenly come together in their teens. For others, it doesn't happen until adulthood. As long as they keep chugging along and are showing effort, we should be patient. Let's look for improvement. It may be slow, but if it's mostly forward motion, we are making progress. I always remind myself that as a child I certainly didn't master a task the first time. Let's set reasonable goals. Then let's look at accomplishing those goals with incremental steps. For example, we want our children to be independent in their self-care.

Independence is a huge goal. But it starts with baby steps: putting their socks on, buttoning their shirt, and so on.

Nothing stagnates progress like an "I can't" attitude. *The Little Engine That Could* should be required reading for every family.[2] Even before they can say, "I can't," some little ones make this helpless noise that sounds something like "Uh." They look up at you with mournful eyes and hand you the trash you know they are able to place in the bin. They act helpless so that you do what they don't want to do. We need to persist with them, to move from "I can't" to "You can learn" to "You will."

Just as we set incremental goals, we also discipline incrementally. We ensure they know what is required, and we are sure they are capable of the work. Next, we give a verbal warning. The next infraction would demand they make right what they have done wrong. For poor quality work, don't make a fuss, just make them go back and improve on their work. If it's habitual, then it is their choice to spend so much time doing shoddy work in the first place when they know they have to repeat the process until they get it right. The key is to not give up, because that is what they are hoping you will do. Persist until they learn to do it right the first time around. It might be necessary to impinge on some fun things they have planned. For example, explain to Christopher, "I know this is the third time you are tidying your room, but your friends will just have to come back another day." If they still aren't cooperating, have them work extra alongside you until they decide to do quality work the first time.

Action Speaks Louder Than Yelling
If words don't work, pain may be necessary for growth. We try to cajole them into obedience. We threaten in order to sound strong, hoping they will obey so we don't have to carry out our threat, because we really don't want to—why can't they just obey? But they know we

---

2. Watty Piper, *The Little Engine That Could* (New York: Grosset & Dunlap, 2020).

won't, so they don't. We can yell at them to hurry up and get ready for school: "The bus is coming! Get your boots on! Where's your backpack?" Or we can calmly say, "If you miss the bus, you will have to pay Mom for gas and time to take you to school by doing extra work," or "Tomorrow morning you will have to get up ten minutes earlier." You may have warned sixteen-year-old Haley on Monday and again on Wednesday that she can't go out with her friends on Friday unless her room is tidy and clean. She has been fully informed. If the job isn't done and her friends show up, you don't need to get upset; you just need to stand by your words. She might yell, but you don't have to. Let the actions speak. If you master this, your parenting will be much more effective. It is likely that enforcing it early will prevent the situation from repeating itself, *if* you are consistent. In this way, you'll be preparing your children for adult life.

Bear Their Own Consequences
Why are some of our children's behaviors aggravating? Because they happen again and again. Nothing seems to bring change—not instruction, persuasion, frustration, raising our voice, or punishment. So why not just let the chips fall where they may? Just back off, and let them bear their own consequences. Let procrastinators carry their own responsibility as early as possible. After they have been fairly warned, after they have been offered help and refused it, when they continue to procrastinate, let them suffer the natural results of their own behavior. They need to feel the pain. Don't cover for them. If you do, you are an enabler, and they will count on you to bail them out again, and it will never end. I know; I have been there. Let them fall, let them fail, and make them pick themselves up, as young as possible. It's fine to assist and advise when they are putting forth the effort, but only when they are doing as much as possible for themselves.

For laundry, this is the plan I recommend: "Kids, I do laundry Tuesdays and Fridays. I'll wash the clothes that are in the hamper, not the ones on the floor. You help as much as your schedule allows." (Mom decides that.) Then don't remind them. Don't gather the clothes you know they will need from their rooms. The day may come when you hear a loud cry from the other end of the house, "Where is my favorite sweater? I absolutely need it today!" Let the crisis happen; it's how they learn if they choose to not listen. Hand-washing clothes is a useful skill anyway. Some parents require every child to do their own laundry. This seems inefficient to me—a waste of water and excess wear and tear on the appliances. It makes more sense to share the work.

If your children are old enough to work an alarm clock, it's their responsibility to get up on time. There is no need for Mom to go to multiple rooms multiple times, more concerned than the children that they will be late for school or work. If you start young, hope-fully this habit will be entrenched by the teen years when they go through growth spurts and need more sleep and when obedience issues might complicate matters.

Hopefully, we can prevent our children from becoming an "adultolescent," a person in their twenties or thirties who behaves like a teenager. If you are saddled with a grown child who won't work, tough love is needed. The nest has to become uncomfortable enough for them to get out into the work world and carry their own weight. It's fine to assist in the process, but they need to work if they are able. Even if they have physical, mental, or emotional limitations, organizations are available to assist in this process.

Finally, if we start young with allowing natural consequences, both positive and negative, to shape our children's behavior, they will be independent by the time they are adults. I pray that all our chil-dren get to the point where they find great fulfillment in their work.

Chapter 21

Enjoy the Good of Your Labor

King Solomon offers words of wisdom to us and to our children in Ecclesiastes 3. There is a time and a season for everything. Birth and death. Planting and plucking up what was planted. Killing and healing. Breaking down and building up. Weeping and laughing. Mourning and dancing. Casting away stones and gathering them together. Embracing and refraining from embracing. Getting and losing. Keeping and casting away. Rending and sewing. Keeping silence and speaking. Loving and hating. War and peace.

Solomon's vivid comparisons cover the depth and breadth and height of life. Then he asks what we gain from all our labor and toil. He answers in verses 10 through 15. God is in charge of everything. He has determined all events from eternity. God never changes; neither does His counsel. Human affairs change all the time. Deep in our hearts, you and I know eternity is real. God placed that awareness in us. God has a secret will and a revealed will. We are commanded to follow God's revealed will. If we don't, our lives will be distressful and end in hell. If we do, it is because of God's work in us. Though we may experience difficulties, we will rest peacefully in His will. This can only happen if we are saved by grace, by the power of the Holy Spirit, through repentance and faith in the work of Jesus Christ. Then our deepest desire is to walk in His ways. It's like we are resting in the palms of His hands. We can truly enjoy the good of our labor as we eat and drink, knowing it is the gift of God. Food, drink, and material goods are tangible blessings; let's look at these in this chapter—enjoying the good of our labor. And the peace, rest, and enjoyment are intangible blessings; in the next chapter we'll study enjoying our labor itself, keeping in mind there is some overlap between the two.

God's Economics

God's plan for economics is simple. We work so we can eat and have a roof over our head. Since the fall of man, it has been: "In the sweat of thy face shalt thou eat bread" (Gen. 3:19). "The labourer is worthy of his reward" (1 Tim. 5:18).

That's the way our world goes round. One or two parents work to earn a living to support their family. This simple plan fits the family at home as well. A family is a community. Work needs to be done to maintain it. Everyone who enjoys the benefits of the community and is able-bodied must contribute. Of the families I interviewed, those with the strongest work ethic impressed this upon their children. They acknowledged God as the Giver of every single thing they owned. They stressed responsibility for each person to carry their load and to serve each other. The parents valued their children enough to include them in the daily duties of running a household. They knew their children would build life skills and enjoy a sense of accomplishment. Even a toddler can fold washcloths and put dirty clothes in the hamper. If a preschooler is tall enough to reach the counter, he can help clear the supper dishes. A school-age child is able to make her own sandwich even though she may need to clean up her mess. Lists of age-appropriate chores are very helpful.[1]

A business is run by statistics and cold, hard facts. But the business of a family is run by love. The bottom line of a business is profit, but the bottom line of our family is to love God the most and our neighbor as ourselves. We begin with our nearest neighbor, those in our own home. Children are blessed to belong to a family. We wrap

---

1. See the appendix for a list of age-appropriate chores for children.

our arms around them and pour our love into them by preparing them to be independent. They are needed, and not just for utilitarian purposes; they are needed because we love them. Love makes work easier. Bree said, "My reward for working was seeing my mom smile and hearing her express appreciation." Marguerite recalled, "I loved my mom so much, I wanted to make her load lighter." "Love makes duty a pleasure," said Puritan Thomas Watson.[2]

Parents do a ton of work for their children, but they should by no means do it all. Kevin Leman proposes this general rule: "Don't do for children what they can do for themselves." He admits to his talent of acting helpless as a five-year-old, even setting up his older brother to get in trouble for not helping him. He believes "acting helpless is a skillful, manipulative technique, and young children (especially the baby of the family) are very good at it."[3] Our children will balk at boring household tasks countless times. But if we allow their unhappiness to influence us as parents to do the mundane tasks because it's sometimes easier than listening to whining, then we deprive our children of the joy of service and the fruit of a humble heart. Remember, whining needs to be met with more work so that our children realize it's not worth it.

Show appreciation and joy for work well done. Yes, work is a duty, but we aren't robots. Why not infuse happiness into everyday life? Negativity seeps in too easily. Let's try to break through the humdrum and make work pleasant so our children associate work with positivity. We adults are encouraged when our boss recognizes our quality work; children, more so. Some kids get a charge out of checking off a chart, and some get a charge out of being appreciated. Give them both.

Speaking of charts—they are great, but you must keep up on them. The Jones family does charts well. Detailed chores are divided and assigned to members of the family by day, week, and month. They are posted, with the calendar and menu, where everyone can

---

2. Thomas Watson, *A Divine Cordial* (Wilmington, Del.: Sovereign Grace, 1972), 98.

3. Kevin Leman, *Have a New Kid by Friday* (Grand Rapids: Revell, 2008), 161.

see them. Parents and children are equally involved. Each child is expected to do their work thoroughly and check that job off the list. Mom randomly checks for quality work. If it's not up to snuff, they need to go back and do it right. They homeschool, so the housework seamlessly blends with the schoolwork. If they want to go out with their friends, Dad or Mom asks, "Is your work finished?" The key is consistency and backing up the expectation with consequences.

Group rewards sometimes work. Miriam's sister slacked while the whole family cleaned every Saturday morning. The kids couldn't play until all the work was finished. Neighboring families did the same. They'd holler out the front door, "We're done dusting! How far are you?" Miriam did a lot of work for her sister just so they could be done and go play. Sister continued the same behavior into adulthood, and her husband covers for her now. The lesson: if one child slacks, they need to keep working while the others are off to play so they learn responsibility and do their part.

Managing Money
Should we give our children an allowance? If so, how much? Do we pay them for their work? I received a wide variety of answers to these questions. Some parents could not afford to give an allowance but needed their children to work hard around the home and farm to support the family. Some did not give allowance out of the principle that the family shares the work and shares the benefits of food, shelter, and clothing. Some parents paid their children specific amounts for specific jobs. Some gave an allowance for extras like vacation money so the children could learn to make spending decisions. Some gave a large allowance to their teens, then taught budgeting by requiring them to cover all their own expenses (transportation, clothes, recreation, etc.). Some gave an allowance for general household duties and extra pay for large jobs or extra voluntary work.

From the wisdom of friends and from our experience, I would advise to clearly teach your children that, as a family, you work together and receive the benefits together. It might require some stark 2 Thessalonians 3:10 lessons of "No dinner until you pick up your toys." Then just start eating without Junior.

At some point in our children's lives, we need to introduce them to their own cash. We must intentionally train them to manage money early on so they don't spend wildly when they receive a paycheck. Valuable life lessons need to be learned under our roof. Start young. Start gradually as well. If we load up our children with money and toys early on, they will come to expect a continuous and ever-increasing stream. We don't want to spoil our children.

I think some allowance is good. We adults get paid with money; it's a real-life experience. We gave our own children a certain amount per week. It increased every year of age because older children have more expenses. I believe the money should be tied to work, though they shouldn't get money for every little chore. Doing chores is just part of being a family; some of their payment comes in the form of a hot meal and a warm bed.

One advantage of giving an allowance is it gives us leverage. If Dylan took the garbage out but did it with defiance, he doesn't deserve his full allowance. Attitude matters. How much better to learn it at home than to get fired from a job. Melinda is required to maintain her half of the bedroom, but she doesn't mind a mess. Yet sister Natalie is neater by nature and gets tired of the untidiness and cleans the whole room. Melinda finds she lost a bit of allowance to pay Natalie for her work. Quality of work matters. That's life.

An excellent idea is to always have a list of extra work for extra pay. When Ethan desperately wants a new bike, yet he has a decent one and it's not his birthday, just show him the list and let him get to work earning it. It prevents coveting and encourages productivity. If we give our children everything they want, they will expect it and think they deserve it. They won't appreciate it nearly as much as if they worked for it. Ethan will take better care of the bike he earned than the one that was given to him. Some families give extra pay for extra work for big jobs that the family does together, like deep cleaning the house in the summer.

If your children have their own business idea, discuss it, plan for it, and go for it if it's reasonable. Get excited with them! The Smiths live next to a golf course, and once a week they take their sons, ages four and eight, to collect stray golf balls. They wash and bag them, and their cousin, who lives on a busy road, sells them on a stand. They all split the profits. Last summer, each boy got $300, half of which went immediately into the bank.

From age nine to fifteen, our children delivered a weekly newspaper. Then they found other jobs. My brother worked on a farm at fourteen and learned diligence and persistence with repetitive tasks. Working for someone else takes the principles learned at home and applies them "out there" working for another boss. Having a "real job" gives a child worth and motivation. You may be concerned about their motivation at home, but they may be diligent on the job. You might even be among the many parents whose child goes off to their first job, and after a few weeks or months, they run into their child's boss and are shocked when the boss says, "Your child is the best worker on my crew." I'm not sure what the psychological processes are, but I think it might have something to do with wanting to prove themselves to the boss and taking ownership and pride in the quality of their work.

A Budgeting Plan

We followed a budgeting system learned from friends. I would go to the bank with our children to cash their paychecks. At home, we would divide their allowance and earnings into categories and record it in a little notebook for each child. The first 10 percent always went to tithing—it's nonnegotiable, lifelong. We can do more with 90 percent with God's blessing than with 100 percent of our money without it.

A young lady once sought counsel of my husband. She was feeling guilty about not tithing. So, she resolved to change. The next Sunday, the offering plate was coming around, and she panicked. She had a one-dollar bill and a twenty-dollar bill, her only cash until the next paycheck. "Which one shall I give?" she asked herself. At the last second, she threw in the $20. The next day, her boss called her into the office. Her heart was racing. She thought, "I only have $1 to my name, and I'm going to lose my job!" But her boss said, "You've been doing such a great job that I'm going to give you a raise." Over the course of the year, the raise added up to $10,000! She certainly felt God's blessing on her giving. Both my husband and I and many others we know have had similar experiences.

It's no secret God promises to bless our tithing. In fact, He challenges us. "Bring ye all the tithes into the storehouse, that there may be meat in mine house, and prove me now herewith, saith the LORD of hosts, if I will not open you the windows of heaven, and pour you out a blessing, that there shall not be room enough to receive it" (Mal. 3:10). You don't want to miss out on this blessing with your children!

In our system, 35 percent went into savings, stashed away in the bank—out of sight, out of mind. This money went toward either college or marriage. You might research investment options with your children because youth savings accounts yield a few pitiful pennies in interest. For each of our children, we also set aside a certain amount of money in a Coverdell Education Savings Account. It ended up covering about one year of university. (For the rest of their tuition, we strongly urged them to keep up their grades and extracurriculars and apply for scholarships.)

Since our city has a number of colleges and universities, we insisted the kids live at home during those years to save money and to stay connected to the church family but, especially, to continue to have conversations about what they were learning. We have heard too many stories of liberal professors who intentionally challenge Christian students and their beliefs to test their faith, or worse, to strip them of their Christian beliefs.

I can't emphasize enough—it is crucial our children learn to save money. Some children are spenders, and some are savers by nature, but spenders still *must* learn to save. Their life and maybe even their future marriage will suffer if they don't. Children are watching our example closely. Have some dinner discussions about the amount of time it takes to earn money, and how quick and easy it is to spend it. When it's spent, it's gone. Poof! Evaporated—especially if the purchase was something edible. Tell them how many hours Daddy has to work to buy a new couch, then say, "That's why we save up for stuff, we plan, and when we buy it, we all try to take good care of it so it lasts."

An extremely important issue to discuss is debt. The vast majority of Americans carry debt; some are almost drowning in it. We are surrounded by advertisements that entice, "No down payment! Wait until next year to pay!" Calculate with your teen the amount you would pay for a car on payments compared to saving and paying cash. Wouldn't they rather have that cash in their own pocket instead of paying a lender? They don't need a fancy first car; they simply need reliable transportation. Student loans are a normal part of life for so many, but evaluate with your child whether there are other ways to pay for university—work, save, and live at home. A wealthy businessman once advised, "The only thing you should go into debt for is a house."

We allowed our children 35 percent for spending. It was their choice, though we did give them guidance, especially when they were young. They usually put a lot of care into the decisions. They bought Legos, scrapbooking supplies, a harp, hunting equipment, and art and sewing supplies. Food and drink are fun, but we tried to influence them to be moderate.

The remaining 20 percent varied over the years. Since my husband is a minister and theologian who loves books, 5 to 10 percent went toward religious books. He would take them over to Reformation Heritage Books and help them choose. We also gave them many books as gifts. By the time they got married, they had a basic library. I highly recommend this. Clothing took 5 to 10 percent. Our kids weren't crazy about that one, but we wanted them to feel responsible. We added to that amount, of course, but some friends turned that category totally over to their teens. Thrift stores and garage sales were their destination. As our children approached driving age, 10 percent went to transportation—gas and saving for a car. They used much of their spending money on transportation as well.

I would recommend involving your children in your own budgeting and home management. Take them along when you purchase a new appliance so they can witness the decision-making process. Discuss future plans over dinner: "This year we hope to fix the retaining wall; we can do that together. Next year, we hope to add a sunroom." Show them how you balance your checkbook, pay utilities, prepare your taxes, and organize your documents. Guide them as they set up their own system. You will give them a head start on running a household wisely.

Opinions vary on sending our children out into the work world. Some parents fear the negative sinful effect of peers in a secular workplace, so they keep their children, especially, girls in the protected environment of the home. My husband and I personally believe it is best to prayerfully and diligently prepare them for the work world and then send them out with guidance, while keeping in close communication with them and praying for God's protection. And beyond that, praying for them to be a witness for Jesus Christ to a hurting and fallen world. Are we guaranteed safety? No, I'm afraid not. But then, nowhere is perfectly safe. Holding down a part-time job while in high school has many benefits. Our children learn to respect figures of authority other than us parents, church leaders, and teachers. They discover how the work world works, and they continue learning to work. They become skilled at managing money. They take on new responsibilities. Working at least forty hours a week during the summer prepares them for adulthood. And they gain experience in working cooperatively with others. Some possible places to work are farms, restaurants, grocery stores, and retail shops; other feasible jobs for teens include lawn care and snow plowing, landscaping, building, cleaning, babysitting, food service worker or nurse's aide in an elder care home, and painting.

We have seen how God gives us the gift of work as well as the rewards that follow. Let's pray our children experience these tangible blessings of enjoying the good of all their labors, because it is a gift of God.

Chapter 22

Enjoy Your Labor

We depend on the tangible blessings of work to live—money, food, and shelter. They are God's gift to us. Providing those needs are met, the *intangible* blessings find a deeper place in our hearts. Let's strive to give our children a taste of the fulfillment and satisfaction of work. These are also a gift of God. The naturally industrious child will taste them sooner and more easily than the resistant child, but we need to press through the haze of laziness, whining, selfishness, boredom, and disobedience to force these blessings upon them. There is no easy way to attain them; the only path is through good, hard work. What are these intangible blessings?

Fulfillment and Joy
I am writing this book during the 2020 pandemic of COVID-19 because all our conference trips were canceled. I have extra time, and my husband challenged me to turn my brainstorming into a book. Currently, millions are out of work or are working from home, and children are not able to go to school for fear of spreading this contagious virus. But other kinds of "viruses" have arisen. Headlines are telling us of significant rises in depression, anxiety, substance abuse, domestic abuse, and suicide. Our mental health suffers when we are not able to carry out our God-given mandate to work. Family members get frustrated with each other. We have too much time and too

few duties to fill it. We lose our sense of purpose. It's not good. This dramatic negative situation only highlights the positive effects that doing work has on all of us.

I believe that very young children have a natural sense of joy in work. They search for things to be happy about. They see adults working, and they want to feel grown up. Why else would there be such a big industry of toys like play fire trucks, kitchens, lawn mowers, and vacuum cleaners? I had an experience a couple months ago that illustrates this.

We live right next to the seminary of which my husband is president. In front of our house is "Puritan Village," where fifty-three people—seminary students and their families—live. I was spreading mulch, and I heard little voices say, "Mrs. Beeke, your house is on fire!" Panicked, I looked at our roof, and to my relief, they continued, "Just pretend! We'll put it out!" So they did, with their pretend hoses. One asked, "Do you have real hoses?"

"Yes."

"Can we use them?"

"Well, I was going to wash our van, so I will get them out soon, after I finish this little job."

"Can we help you?"

"Sure!"

I didn't want to discourage youthful initiative. They were so eager, I had to take turns between the three boys and the three girls putting handfuls of mulch in the flower beds. Next, I got the soap and hose out and backed up the van as their moms had them sit on the grass. They helped me hose down the van—all six of them, ages two to five, like firefighters lined up. They observed the rainbow from the water spraying in the sunshine. Thankfully, I had five mitts and a sponge, so they all took a section and sponged down the van. We rinsed it and dried it. When we were finished, one of the boys asked, "Can I plant a garden with you?" The temperature was pushing ninety degrees, so I responded, "Let's do that another time."

I couldn't stop smiling. Their ambition was bursting out. Their imaginations weren't being stymied sitting in front of a screen. By starting young with our children and setting a tone of enjoying work, by having fun together, by celebrating with them, we can ride this wave of energy as long as it lasts. They might decide later that work is tedious, but we'll deal with that when it happens. That morning those six kids learned how to spread mulch and wash a vehicle, and they had the satisfaction of accomplishing work and helping a neighbor.

Purpose and Worth

Working makes us feel worthwhile. When Harper runs to get a washcloth for Mommy, who is bathing baby Simon, she knows she has purpose. There was a need, and she filled it. The littlest child senses this, especially when Mommy thanks her "big girl." We do our children great favors when we involve them in the daily duties of home life. We need them, and it's good for them to feel needed. Dad takes the kids along to the home improvement store Saturday morning to buy a swing set. They assemble it together and get the reward of swinging and sliding. Not only are they invested in the family and their possessions but they also learned "righty-tighty, lefty-loosey" as they helped Dad turn the wrench.

Rotating chores gives broad experience to each child. But when they find a certain niche, they take pride in their specialty. I still feel good about being the one who fried the bacon, made the frosting, and helped Dad move the table saw when I was a kid. Friends of ours share common labor around their home, but the son who is gifted at understanding computers is tasked with solving tech problems, and the daughter who enjoys culinary adventures often cooks special suppers.

Involving all our children in meal planning and preparation is an adventure with fun rewards. Who doesn't enjoy eating? Why not expand our children's horizons into the culinary world? They will learn responsibility and survival skills. Because she had trained them, Terri's teenagers were capable of cooking and running the household when she needed to care for her aging mother in another state for two weeks. They also witnessed her dedication and were privileged to participate in the sacrifice and service.

Accomplishment

It's just a really good feeling when we accomplish a task. After we have worked hard and done quality work, we have a God-given sense of satisfaction inside. This proves God designed us for work. "The sleep of a labouring man is sweet" (Eccl. 5:12). You know it. Let's ensure our children experience this too. Don't let them give up. Cleaning the bathroom, building a model airplane, sweeping the garage, finishing that difficult math assignment, painting a room, growing and selling microgreens—whether it's mundane or exciting, big or small, when it's finished they'll have a sense of achievement. Even unpleasant jobs afford us this sense, maybe more so, because their unpleasantness makes the job more challenging. Plus, if we don't enjoy the work itself, we will be *very* happy when it's done!

By requiring our children to work, we gift them with skills, knowledge, confidence, and problem-solving capabilities. They are learning to be dependable and responsible. They are becoming equipped for adult life, wherever the Lord will lead. It's a good thing worth working for.

Our children can be programmed to follow the entitlement culture of our day. But being handed something without earning it or, worse, demanding something someone else has earned leaves us empty. A natural dignity mounts in our children's hearts when they do honest work for honest pay. And when they experience it, they will want more.

Perseverance

Some children have genetics of diligence, organization, and perseverance. But some don't. We parents will encounter crying, stonewalling, procrastination, and plain old disobedience. We must persevere with the work of parenting so that our children learn to persevere in their work. I have simple advice—stick to your guns. Plan carefully. You know when to expect a battle. So make sure your demands are realistic, because once you have laid them on the table, you *must* follow through. Don't waver; convey the expectation that *they will work.* If you don't win, you lose. And they win. Then they will be strengthened for the next battle, and you will be in a weaker position of disadvantage.

Persevere with this picture in mind—see your child working diligently and enjoying the satisfaction of a job well done. Just imagine your child as an adult thanking you for your persistence so that they could be equipped for a successful career. We show our love to our children by *not* allowing their protests to win the day. Press on. Make them work. It is good for them. Yes, it's easier to do it yourself, and sometimes you will just do that. But if you have told them to do a job, then make sure they do it thoroughly. They may collapse, they may scream, they may say it's not fair, but be strong. You need to persevere so that *they* learn to persevere. They will eventually learn to be responsible, and their conscience will be clear when they obey. They'll respect themselves and will have peace in their heart. It may take years, but wait for it—it will come.

Appreciation and Loyalty

When our children cooperate and work well, it is a joyful thing, and we should affirm them. We shouldn't take it for granted, even though obedience is required. Let's reinforce it until it becomes a way of life. If we convey a begrudging attitude of "Well, that's what they are supposed to do anyway. They don't need a reward or thanks," we miss opportunities to instill joy into work and strengthen our relationship with our children. We don't need to jump for joy or pay cash for every little thing they do, but appreciation builds respect. We teach them to say "Please" and "Thank you," and we say the same words to them.

As they grow up and become more proficient, we dial down the reinforcement so they realize work is expected of them, and they grow up into other intangible rewards. It shows love and humility to serve each other and to be grateful for our family members' service to us.

Duty sounds like drudgery. It can be, but it doesn't have to be. Duty is good. It is defined as something we are morally expected to do, a task that we do to show respect to others. I would suggest that duty is closely tied to loyalty. Both bind us together as family and society. Duty drives us to care for each other, even when the task is unpleasant, just *because* we care for and love one another. Children can be taught duty—setting the table, serving a snack, or picking beans. The work simply has to be done.

Loyalty can lead to a legacy. As you build family loyalty by working together and serving each other, you are establishing habits that will be passed down through the generations. Tell your children stories about their heritage as you eat dinner or travel. After my grandparents passed away, our whole family divided their belongings. I was privileged to receive the wooden toolbox Grandpa Kamp carried his carpentry tools in as he worked around town. For years I used it to hold my garden tools, but it is weakening, so I plan to give it a place of greater honor and make a centerpiece out of it. I also have the enamelware-top table that Grandma Kamp preserved fruits and vegetables on. I love to tell our children and grandchildren stories about their work, how Grandpa straightened the nails from the old chicken coop and reused them for the new one. Or how Grandma was known as the "egg lady" to the neighbors. Our legacy molds us. Let's preserve it and pass it on to our children.

Sharing

Tangible blessings blend with the intangible. Let's teach our children to work hard to earn money and rewards. But let's also teach them to share their belongings, and they will experience more joy than they could imagine. There is no happiness in selfishness. It's a train that leads to nowhere. And the train must be derailed. Start young. Selfishness surfaces in toddlers. The moment we notice it is the moment we steer them in a different direction. Mason grabs his brother's truck. Calmly coach him to give it back. "You can have it when Elijah is finished with it." Distract him with another toy. Praise him when he cooperates. We replace selfishness with selflessness by not giving our children everything their little hearts desire. Saying no builds their character.

The shallow joy of obtaining stuff and keeping it for ourselves is nothing compared with the deep joy of sharing with others. Emma comes home from a birthday party. Brother Tyler looks longingly at the goodie bag. Encourage Emma to give some to Tyler. Thank Emma for her kindness, and point out how happy she made Tyler. We may have exaggerated the praise and gratitude to our children when they shared, but I think it worked. Sometimes we would physically pry the coveted item out of one child's hand. By demonstrating the action and explaining how they *should* be feeling, then reinforcing the joy when they obeyed, they learned to share willingly. Let's implant this desire in their hearts, so that when they reach adulthood, they will generously support the church and their needy neighbor.

The rich young ruler didn't learn this lesson as a child. He obeyed God's commandments, and he must have worked hard and earned a lot of money. But when he inquired about eternal life, Jesus told him, "One thing thou lackest: go thy way, sell whatsoever thou hast, and give to the poor, and thou shalt have treasure in heaven: and come, take up the cross, and follow me" (Mark 10:21). He walked away very sad, unaware of the great joy he had just passed up. When we know the Lord, we will want to share.

Empathy
Empathy can also be learned at a young age. Some children have it naturally. The rest need to be taught. Some are born compassionate. Others may need to catch it by Mom suggesting, "Your brother is

working hard out in the garage; let's bring him a snack!" or "Let's surprise Mommy and get the kitchen clean and tidy by the time she gets home!"

The Golden Rule is truly golden. A child may be able to express his or her feelings, or you might need to draw them out. When they understand their own feelings, tell them others feel that way too. "Remember when Charlotte next door grabbed the best toys for herself and wouldn't share? Remember, you were sad and mad. That is what you are doing right now with your sister." Make them share so they can experience the gratification that comes with it. Point out how sister's tears changed to a smile when she shared. Then her joy will take the place of selfish desires. Will they learn instantly? Probably not, but persist, and it will happen.

Our example is paramount. Give a snack, a gift card, and a Bible to a homeless person begging by an intersection. Give to worthy charities. Donate stuff you don't need to a thrift shop or to a neighbor in need. Share your heritage; if you are a two-parent family, take your crew to help a single-parent family. Have the kids work together, and they can all learn. And express the joy that comes with it. "God loveth a cheerful giver" (2 Cor. 9:7).

Service

Perhaps the greatest intangible blessing of work is when we and our children serve others. Grace was born with various impairments, even though she seemed completely normal and healthy at birth. Her complications were not discovered until she was four months old. Grace has grown into a very happy, social, energetic, fun-loving, and love-giving teenager. She has required much care from each member of her family, her special education school, and numerous medical specialists and therapists. Her family has met this huge challenge with truckloads of love. You might think her older siblings would be ready to escape the world of special needs when they went out on their own. But no, Grace's two older sisters have both pursued careers in caring for handicapped children. They have experienced the deep joy that comes with helping others in need. There are really no words to describe this feeling of worthwhileness.

If you take away nothing else from this book, take this: give your children the inestimable privilege of serving others. Start young so that this joy is woven into the very fiber of their being. Bake cookies and bring them to the lady with cancer in your church. Have your children shovel an elderly neighbor's driveway every time it snows. Stay after church gatherings, and involve the whole family in the cleanup. Rescue a puppy and adopt him. Serve each other in the family, especially siblings, because at times they are the ones they might be least inclined to want to serve.

You might be asking, "*Make* them serve?" That's a contradiction in terms. Serving isn't serving if it's forced. True. But we make them do many things they don't want to do, and we trust that over time they will experience the internal rewards. Then they will serve from their hearts and will never want to stop. We train the behavior and pray the motives fall in place.

Serving must be a lifestyle. Set the example, and pray your children will carry on this legacy. Steer them to a career of service. But no matter what occupation they choose, we trust they have an attitude of "What can I do to help whomever I meet on the pathway of life?" And prepare yourselves for great blessings.

Ultimately, the greatest joy in work is found in serving God from a heart that loves God. Unbelievers can enjoy their work very much, but believers have a deeper joy, even if they are doing menial labor. We were created to work, and we were created for God's glory, so our work glorifies Him. His love motivates us to serve Him; we know our work is not in vain. We recognize that we have purpose, and that gives us profound satisfaction.

Furthermore, our love for God overflows in the form of love to our neighbor. Jesus rewarded those who fed Him when He was hungry, gave Him a drink when He was thirsty, clothed Him when He was naked, took Him in as a stranger, and visited Him while sick and imprisoned. They were surprised that He honored them, and asked when they did these things. He replied, "Verily I say unto you, Inasmuch as ye have done it unto one of the least of these my brethren, ye have done it unto me" (Matt. 25:40).

If we are believers, we will serve the underprivileged. How exciting to do this with our children by our side! It's a triple reward. We pour ourselves out for our needy neighbor, and we are happy they are more comfortable. We experience the intense joy in our own hearts that comes with serving. And we exemplify serving to our children. They will catch it! We have an opportunity to start them on a lifelong adventure of serving their neighbor, of living a life with deep purpose and great joy. How exciting if we witness the Lord's saving work in our children and see their growth in grace as they love their neighbor as themselves.

Conclusion

I conclude with a story. There once were two elderly rich men. One gave generously to causes that promoted the gospel. The other gave very little, though he always promised to give more in the future. The generous man told his friend, "You will give your money with a cold hand, but I have the joy and blessing of giving with a warm hand." Don't wait until you die to share your possessions with good causes. Don't even wait until you have extra. Trust and obey. Teach your children *now*, and show them how "it is more blessed to give than to receive" (Acts 20:35).

Chapter 23

Rest and Perfect Work

Let me put into a nutshell what I have been saying about teaching our children to work and building a positive work ethic in them:

- Entreaty: Pray for God's wisdom and blessing as you teach your children to work. Let love for God and your children rule your parenting.

- Example: Work hard so they follow your example of diligence. Demonstrate life skills along the pathway of everyday life.

- Expectation: Your children sense your attitude. Expect them to work, and deal calmly and decisively with resistance.

- Early education: Begin young. They are able. They are a contributing member of the family. Work is part of life. Work is good.

- Enjoyment: Work is fulfilling and rewarding. Your positive attitude will rub off on them. Work brings joy. Enjoy the good of your labors.

- Excitement: Share your excitement about the potential of what your children can accomplish.

- Encouragement: Encourage and thank your children for their work. It builds a positive attitude.

- Exhortation: You will need to exhort and discipline your children as you train them to work. Prepare a plan of action to back up your rules.

- Emptiness: An attitude of entitlement leaves a person empty.

- Equipping: Working at home equips your child for adult life. Train them in a wide variety of skills. Give many experiences; some may lead to their career.

- Earnings: Working earns money. Make sure they learn and experience this.

- Emotions: Consider emotions when teaching your children to work, but don't let emotions rule.

- Experience: Ensure your children experience the sense of accomplishment and satisfaction that comes with a job well done.

- Effort: Recognize effort. Aim for improvement, not perfection. Have age-appropriate expectations.

- Energy: As a family, approach work with energy and eagerness as much as is physically possible.

- Endurance: Work can be exhausting. But with God's grace and strength, you can endure!

- Empathy: Show empathy and love to your children; be firm, but don't be a taskmaster. Teach empathy to them by serving others together.

Life isn't all about work. God built us to rest also. We take time to eat, take breaks from work, and enjoy recreation. Children play many hours. Eight, ten, or twelve (for children) hours out of each day are for sleeping and recharging our batteries. One day out of each week is for resting from our labors. God set that pattern in creation. After creating the heavens and the earth, He rested from His work, though He didn't need to. He sanctified and blessed the seventh day (Ex. 20:8–11). He set it aside for our sake so that we could rest our bodies and worship Him. We need physical rest *and* spiritual rest. We do well to follow this ordinance that dates all the way back to the beginning of the world. It's God's gift to us. Since Christ died and then arose on the first day of the week, He set the pattern for the day of rest and worship to be on Sunday. When we let our frenzied lifestyle spill over into the Lord's Day, we shortchange ourselves of peace and rest. When we abbreviate our worship of the God who made us and gave us everything we've ever had, we shortchange ourselves of sweet blessings. Isaiah 58:13–14 contrasts the blessings we receive when we delight in God and honor Him on His day, with the sin of using the Lord's Day for our own pleasure. God's schedule is best for us and our children.

Life is short and eternity is long. We and our children need to be ready to meet God. If we die unprepared, we will spend forever in the torments of hell. "What must I do to be saved?" pleaded the Philippian jailor. Paul and Silas answered, "Believe on the Lord Jesus Christ, and thou shalt be saved" (Acts 16:30–31).

When we have truly repented of our sins and been washed in the blood of Jesus Christ, we are prepared to meet God, and we will spend eternity with Him. What is heaven like? It's a mixture of rest and holy activity. God's people will "rest from their labours" (Rev. 14:13). It will be an eternal Sabbath or rest. We will share in the glory and love of our Savior, Jesus Christ (John 17:24). Paul anticipated receiving a crown of righteousness as a gracious reward for all his missionary work (2 Tim. 4:7–8). Jesus comforts and assures us there are many mansions, or rooms, for us in heaven, and that He went ahead to prepare a place for us (John 14:1–3). We will be home. We will have peace and no pain (Rev. 21:4). We won't be burdened anymore by the thorns and thistles. The Lamb will feed us and lead us to living fountains of water (Rev. 7:17). Jesus Christ is the King of heaven, and we will reign forever with Him (Rev. 21:3–5).

The crowning activity of heaven will be the worship of God. The Lord Jesus Christ will be on the throne in the center, and we will praise Him for His work of creation and redemption (Rev. 4:2, 8, 9; 5:9). The redeemed will worship Him and sing, "Great and marvellous are thy works, Lord God Almighty; just and true are thy ways, thou King of saints" (Rev. 15:3). We will have joyful fellowship with angels, saints, and, best of all, with Jesus Christ Himself. It will be an eternity of praise-centered rest and thorn-free work!

Study Questions

Introduction: How Work Began

1. What were mankind's first assignments for work? What practical lessons can we learn from Adam's first tasks?

2. What does it mean in Genesis 2:15 that Adam and Eve were charged to dress and keep the garden?

3. What can we learn from the fact that work was assigned to man before the fall when everything was perfect, peaceful, and beautiful?

4. How can you use the idea that work was a beautiful gift of God sanctioned by Him before the fall to teach both yourself and your children (1) about the attitude that we should have toward work and (2) about the value of work?

5. What punishments did God deliver to Adam? To Eve? How would it affect relationships between God and Adam and Eve?

6. How did God show mercy? Do you find this amazing? In what ways? How could we explain this to our children? Make a short list of the sad parts of this story and contrast them with the hopeful parts. What is your hope?

7. How does God's work differ from ours? What are the facets of God's work? What does each one mean to you?

8. What are the facets of man's work? Give an example of each.

9. In light of the environmental movement of today, how would you present to your teens a balanced, biblical approach to subduing the earth and exercising dominion over creatures?

10. Name some examples of burdens of work. Which ones are the most burdensome for you? For your children?

11. What blessings of work do unbelievers experience? What is God's aim as He deals with them?

12. In what ways do believers experience greater blessings and joy in their work than unbelievers? How could you explain and demonstrate this difference to your children? How do you view your work in light of God's place in your life?

Chapter 1: Work Is Good for Kids

1. What was your experience, in relation to work, growing up? What is your view on making children work? What are some extremes to watch out for?

2. List five types of play and the benefits that come with them.

3. Why is it important to take years to transition from a life of mostly play to mostly work? Give some examples of what this might look like.

4. What are some benefits of starting young with teaching work skills? Name some tasks little children can perform.

5. What are your goals for your children to learn in two years? In four years?

Chapter 2: Foundations

1. In what ways is truth so vital as we teach our children to work? Give several examples.

2. Why is it essential that we glorify God in all that we do? How can we do this with our children as we teach them to work?

3. How can we demonstrate love to God in our homes?

4. What does love to our neighbor look like in everyday clothes? How do you live this out in your family?

5. The Scriptures are full of wisdom. Look up *wisdom* in a concordance, and choose two favorite verses on this subject. Explain their meaning and how you would teach them to your children.

6. Why is holiness so important for us to pursue? What are practical ways to promote it in our homes?

Chapter 3: It's in the Atmosphere

1. In a generic sense, list some home atmospheres that are positive and some that are negative. Evaluate the atmosphere of your own home. What are you doing well? How can you challenge yourself to improve?

2. Why is love so important? How can we nurture love in our own hearts and in the hearts of our children?

3. How can we encourage our children in their work?

4. Think of examples where we need to show tough love to our children. What biblical principles should we remember when we chastise our children for their good but they see it differently?

5. How do our children respond to our example? Describe two situations in which your example positively influenced your child to work. List one way you can set an example for your child in the future.

6. If you have an expectation that your children will work, how will this manifest itself in your attitude and words? What are some constructive ways to convey this attitude to your children?

Chapter 4: Subdue Their Will to Set Them Free

1. What does Scripture teach us about a child's will? Why is it so important to have a proper perspective on this?

2. Give three examples of how we can begin to mold our child's will when they are a baby or a toddler. Why is it essential to deal with defiance early?

3. What are the dangers of not recognizing our children's sin nature?

4. Seeing our child as a sinner seems to contradict with the command to love them. How can we reconcile these? How is the gospel of Jesus Christ connected to this?

5. Why is it important to mix encouragement with discipline? How can we train our child's will while showing them respect? How can we subdue their will while not breaking their spirit?

6. List three helpful principles for handling the strong-willed child.

Chapter 5: Turn Over the Reins

1. In a few words, describe each of these: self-discipline, self-control, and self-respect. Give an example of each. Why are they important for training our children to work?

2. What are the benefits of maintaining a positive attitude while teaching our children to work? What challenges do we face? What verses from Scripture encourage you?

3. Think of four basic skills our children need to learn to be on their way to becoming independent. How would you recommend teaching them?

4. How do you know when your child has mastered a skill and turned it into a habit? List two bad habits you are trying to prevent your child from developing and two good ones you are building. How do habits take time and save time?

5. Think back to your growing up years. How did you grow in confidence in working in the home? How did your parents teach you independence? What are your plans for building confidence and teaching independence to your children?

6. What are the advantages to having your child trained to be independent by the time they are a teen? What struggles might you encounter in the teen years? How will you meet these struggles?

7. What is your identity as a worker? In other words, how would you fill in this blank, "I am a _____ worker"? What kind of an identity are you building in your child?

Chapter 6: Custom Training

1. In what ways do we need to rear our children all alike? In what ways should we rear them differently from each other?

2. What are the seven widely accepted learning styles? What is yours? What are your children's learning styles?

3. What are the four work styles described? What is your work style? Your children's?

4. From your life experience, can you suggest more learning styles and work styles? Why should we be careful about putting our children into tidy little boxes?

5. Why is it necessary for us as parents to discipline our children? Give scriptural support from Proverbs or elsewhere.

6. Give some examples of how to exercise discipline according to the character of a child. What are some ways to prevent the need to discipline?

Chapter 7: Together Time

1. What are your thoughts on children working in the home? What obstacles do you encounter? How will you overcome them?

2. Give some examples of appropriate work for little children. What are the pros and cons of having little ones work with you?

3. From "We Are in This Together," what principles from the previous chapters of this book do you see applied here?

4. The couple in "Looking Back" has both positive thoughts and regrets about their family story. How do you see their story? What practices would you follow in your family?

5. In "Multitasking," what is it about the parents' example and attitude that makes the children work? How do they deal with resistance to work? What are your thoughts on forcing our children to work?

6. What lessons have you learned from this chapter? How would you like to implement them?

Chapter 8: Don't Spare for Their Crying

1. What does the first part of Proverbs 19:18 mean? What are the two possible interpretations of the second part?

2. Do any of the behaviors listed under "Heading in the Wrong Direction" sound familiar? What could you add to the list? Which ones do you need to work on in your children?

3. What must happen in the child's mind for him or her to change their attitude and their behavior?

4. What steps should a parent who is dealing with the behaviors listed in this chapter take? What scriptural verses would be encouraging? Write out a prayer for this parent to pray.

5. Why are planning and perseverance so important for success in this struggle? What place do patience and love have?

6. Give an example of a child resisting work in some way, and offer a plan for dealing with it.

Chapter 9: Praying and Thinking

1. What is it about teaching our children to work that can be frustrating? List three factors.

2. What is so special and important about prayer? Share with others how God has answered a prayer of yours.

3. As parents, why is it beneficial to reason with ourselves? What method do you find most helpful for resolving dilemmas?

4. What are the advantages to thinking in "teacher mode"? What are your thoughts on "be a robot (or not)"?

5. What visual pictures help you to cope with the frustrations of teaching your children to work?

6. What are the advantages of keeping our own emotions in control?

Chapter 10: Monitor Screen Time

1. From your life experience, what are the benefits of technology? What are the dangers? How has technology impacted your family?

2. From the research described in this chapter, list three positive results of our children's interaction with media. How can this help them in their future careers?

3. What special warnings do secular scientists give for babies and young children being exposed to media? How do these little ones learn best?

4. What specific dangers are associated with video games?

5. How does overuse of technology affect a child's brain and thinking? What other factors in the home contribute to overuse?

6. Habits can lead to addiction. How does addiction affect the brain? How does addiction to technology impact other areas of life?

7. List and describe two scars our children can experience from misuse or overuse of technology. In what ways do you find these troubling?

8. How important is it for us as parents to know what technology is entering our children's lives and to be in control of it? How can we accomplish this? How can we use it as a tool that we control and not allow it to control us?

9. How should we talk to our children about the use of technology? Give examples of a conversation with a seven-year-old and a thirteen-year-old. How can we blend positives with the warnings?

10. Write up a plan for technology use for your family.

Chapter 11: Good No Matter What

1. When you think about good things, what comes to mind? What picture comes to mind of your child as an adult in the work world doing good?

2. Which commandments have a direct connection to work? Explain how they are connected, and give an example.

3. Why is it so important that our children have God's Word written on their hearts by the time they are adults? What benefits do we give our children when we catch them doing wrong?

4. We enrich our children when we provide experiences of doing good to others. What are some examples of how we can do this as a family?

5. How can we nurture in our children a desire to do good to others, whether it be as a hero, in a career that helps and serves, or just in small ways in the course of everyday life?

6. What is a biblically balanced attitude for our children to strive for in the area of building a good reputation?

Chapter 12: Work Is What We Do

1. Children come in a million varieties. Describe two or three children you know who approach work in different ways. What is your own approach to work?

2. How do some children try to wriggle out of work? What are their thoughts and their actions? How should we respond?

3. Why do children have to learn to do mundane tasks? How do we train them in boring, repetitious chores?

4. What rewards do children experience when they accept mundane tasks and become proficient in their work?

5. Why is work before play a good idea? What comparisons does Elisabeth Elliot make? What is your experience in this area?

Chapter 13: Let's Go

1. What is the effect of momentum in work? Share some experiences you have had personally or with your children.

2. Define the different types of inertia. How do they relate to our children working?

3. What are some hindrances to the inertia of work? How can we overcome these hindrances? What word pictures might motivate your child?

4. Forward motion continues the work. How can we keep the pressure on our children to keep working when they want to slow down or stop?

5. What steps can we take when we or our children are prone to indecisiveness or procrastination?

6. What benefits will your child experience in their future occupation if they learn to finish whatever task they start?

Chapter 14: With All Your Might

1. Compare and contrast the biblical perspective on work and wages with an entitlement and socialist perspective. How can we instruct our children biblically?

2. How does working with all our might benefit ourselves? How can we teach diligence to our children? What is the difference between the mindset of children when they are given something compared to when they work for it and earn it?

3. Sometimes there is overlap. How does diligent work, with its rewards, benefit both us and others at the same time?

4. What benefits do our children receive when they work for others? Share an experience you or a family member have had serving others.

5. What is the ultimate reason we and our children are to work heartily? How can we inspire our children to aspire to work for God's glory?

Chapter 15: Work Smart

1. What are the advantages to planning well before you start working? Share an example of doing this with your children.

2. What are some benefits to establishing a routine and following a schedule? What sort of routine do you and your family members follow? How do various individual personalities handle a routine?

3. What special considerations should a parent make for a distractible or a hyperactive child? Can you offer ideas for helping this child work through a task?

4. How do we develop proficiency and expertise in our children? Share some pointers.

5. Why is it good to teach our children to be proactive? Share your ideas about how to do this.

6. Share a unique way that you and your family work smart. How do you teach your children to work smart?

Chapter 16: Overcome Obstacles

1. What do you admire about Joseph as he persevered in the face of difficult providences? What lessons can we and our children learn from him? How can we even be encouraged?

2. From your life experience, how have you seen a roadblock become a ladder? In other words, how have early, difficult life experiences led to a positive outcome?

3. What advice would you give to a teen who is not academically inclined and who finds school challenging but who has vocational skills? What opportunities would you suggest he or she pursue?

4. How does our attitude affect how we handle difficulties? How can we encourage our children to make use of hard times, whether they brought them on themselves or whether they were outside their control? What role does prayer have?

5. When our children have done wrong, they need to learn from their mistakes. What steps do we take to deal with them? What principles do we follow?

6. The greatest blessings that could come out of overcoming hard times are serving others and knowing Jesus Christ. Have you had this experience, or do you know someone who has? Share a story.

Chapter 17: Time Is a Treasure

1. What is your perspective on time? Do you treasure every minute?

2. What is God's perspective on time? What principles should we teach our children about the value of time? What does it mean to redeem time?

3. What is our most urgent, time-sensitive need? Which parts of our week do we devote to seeking God with our family? Briefly write out a schedule for a typical week.

4. What is the difference between idleness and relaxation (or rest)? Challenge yourself to improve your own use of time and your family's.

5. Which of the examples in the section "Practical Ideas on Treasuring Time" resonate with you? What helps you and your family treasure time? Add a story or suggestion of your own.

6. How can we teach our children to work while it is day, for the night is coming, when no man can work? How can we dedicate our time and our life to God?

Chapter 18: Take Care of Your Stuff

1. What are the benefits of neatness? What are the disadvantages of clutter?

2. What is God's perspective on possessions? Choose one of the verses listed, and explain it in a child's terms.

3. How do we, in our hearts and minds, sometimes misuse the gifts God gives us? How does our culture impact us and our children? What verses from Scripture can we use to find a balanced view? Write out a prayer.

4. How can we teach our children to not be selfish? Describe a sensible attitude toward stuff for a child.

5. How can we train our children to take care of their stuff from a young age on into the teen years? What is a good cleaning plan? Share any special tips that have worked well for you.

6. How can we balance taking good care of God's gifts to us with not setting our hearts on them and loving them too much?

Chapter 19: Follow Your Talents

1. Briefly describe the uniqueness of each of your children. What talents do you see in each one?

2. How can you feed your child's interests? How do we help them find a balance between excited dreaming and realism?

3. What dinner discussions could you have that would focus on your children's interests and aspirations that might lead to a future career?

4. Explain the value of your child finding a lower-level job in the field of their interest.

5. Tell a story of how someone has inspired or influenced you or a loved one to follow a particular occupation. If possible, have your teens shadow you, your spouse, or someone else on the job. Who could your teen interview to find out more about a potential career?

6. God's providence is our pathway in life. God knows the end from the beginning. Is this comforting or frightening? Write a brief prayer for your children to find and follow their talents.

Chapter 20: Natural Consequences

1. How is Newton's third law connected to children learning to work? How have you implemented this in your home? How do children understand this law even before they can talk or walk?

2. What are natural consequences? Why are negative natural consequences necessary?

3. Describe the best emotional frame of mind to be in when we discipline our children. What must be our ultimate goal for our children?

4. What negative emotions must we deal with in ourselves before we discipline? Describe two examples of approaching discipline in a direct but not derogatory tone.

5. What questions should we ask in our mental checklist before we administer discipline?

6. What factors should we consider when deciding on a fitting discipline? Give two examples of a child resisting work and a fitting discipline for it.

7. When we expect our children to learn to work incrementally, what do we look for? How do we overcome an "I can't" attitude?

8. Why is it so important that we allow our actions to speak louder than our yelling? Give an example of this.

9. Describe a situation where a child you know had to learn a lesson by bearing their own consequences. Why do we sometimes need to let them fail?

Chapter 21: Enjoy the Good of Your Labor

1. Who can truly enjoy the good of their labor? Why?

2. What is God's plan for economics? How does this work in society? In the family? What are some benefits to living as a community in our family?

3. What is your perspective on giving an allowance to children? What factors need to be considered? If you have other ideas than the ones described, share them.

4. What should our attitude be to our children when they work well? What are your thoughts on charts? List some pros and cons.

5. What lifelong lessons can children learn from being taught to manage their money?

6. How can you encourage your ambitious child to find creative ways to work extra? How can you help your child start a business?

7. How important is tithing? What blessings does God promise to those who tithe? Privately, challenge yourself and your children to obey God in this way, if you are not at this time.

8. How can we teach our children to save? What is the best way to teach our children to avoid debt as much as possible? How can you teach them to budget?

9. In what ways can we steer our children to make wise choices with their money? What are pros and cons of our children having a job during their high school years?

Chapter 22: Enjoy Your Labor

1. What intangible blessings do we receive from work? Which one resonates with you the most?

2. What is it about work that gives us joy and fulfillment? What gives you this sense? How can we nurture this in our children?

3. Describe your feeling of purpose and worth when you have completed a task. Give an example of your child working and experiencing this in the home.

4. Why is it crucial for us to require our children to do both pleasant and unpleasant tasks? What are the benefits that come with accomplishing a task? Share a story in which you experienced a special sense of accomplishment.

5. What obstacles might you encounter when you try to teach your children perseverance? When they learn perseverance, what benefits will they experience?

6. What good things happen in our family when we appreciate and thank each other? In what ways is duty a good thing? How are duty and loyalty connected? Share a part of your family's legacy.

7. Compare selfishness with selflessness. Where does each one lead to? What techniques would you suggest to teach our children to share?

8. How can empathy be shown in the home as we work for each other?

9. Why is serving others so addicting? How can we model serving to our children so that they adopt a lifestyle of serving? Give an example of how your family serves others.

10. Why is serving God in our work the *best* intangible blessing? Give an example of how you have experienced this joy or how you would like to in the future.

Chapter 23: Rest and Perfect Work

1. Choose three of the words in the list beginning with *E* that mean the most to you, and explain why. Share ways of implementing them in your family.

2. What are the two ways in God's order of creation in which He built rest into our schedules?

3. Why is spiritual rest just as important as physical rest? What happens when we replace worship with work or recreation? What blessings does God promise when we remember the Sabbath day to keep it holy?

4. This book is chiefly about our physical work, but what is the most important work we need God to do in our hearts and in our children's hearts? Privately, make your call and election sure, and pray for His grace to fill your home every day.

5. What are two types of rest we believers will experience in heaven? What is the main activity of heaven? What excites you the most?

Appendix

Age-Appropriate Chores for Children

© Copyright 2013 www.flandersfamily.info

Ages 2-3

- ☐ Put toys in toy box
- ☐ Stack books on shelf
- ☐ Place dirty clothes in laundry hamper
- ☐ Throw trash away
- ☐ Carry firewood
- ☐ Fold washcloths
- ☐ Set the table
- ☐ Fetch diapers & wipes
- ☐ Dust baseboards

Ages 4-5

- ☐ Feed pets
- ☐ Wipe up spills
- ☐ Put away toys
- ☐ Make the bed
- ☐ Straighten bedroom
- ☐ Water houseplants
- ☐ Sort clean silverware
- ☐ Prepare simple snacks
- ☐ Use hand-held vacuum
- ☐ Clear kitchen table
- ☐ Dry and put away dishes
- ☐ Disinfect doorknobs

Ages 6-7

- ☐ Gather trash
- ☐ Fold towels
- ☐ Dust mop floors
- ☐ Empty dishwasher
- ☐ Match clean socks
- ☐ Weed garden
- ☐ Rake leaves
- ☐ Peel potatoes or carrots
- ☐ Make salad
- ☐ Replace toilet paper roll

Ages 8-9

- ☐ Load dishwasher
- ☐ Change light bulbs
- ☐ Wash laundry
- ☐ Hang/fold clean clothes
- ☐ Dust furniture
- ☐ Spray off patio
- ☐ Put groceries away
- ☐ Scramble eggs
- ☐ Bake cookies
- ☐ Walk dogs
- ☐ Sweep porches
- ☐ Wipe off table

Ages 10-11

- ☐ Clean bathrooms
- ☐ Vacuum rugs
- ☐ Clean countertops
- ☐ Deep clean kitchen
- ☐ Prepare simple meal
- ☐ Mow lawn
- ☐ Bring in mail
- ☐ Do simple mending (hems, buttons, etc.)
- ☐ Sweep out garage

Ages 12 and up

- ☐ Mop floors
- ☐ Change overhead lights
- ☐ Wash/ vacuum car
- ☐ Trim hedges
- ☐ Paint walls
- ☐ Shop for groceries w/list
- ☐ Cook complete dinner
- ☐ Bake bread or cake
- ☐ Do simple home repairs
- ☐ Wash windows
- ☐ Iron clothes
- ☐ Watch younger siblings

Source: "Age-Appropriate Chores for Children," Flanders Family Homelife (blog), https://www.flandersfamily.info/web/2013/11/13/age-appropriate-chores-for-children. Permission granted: © 2013 by Jennifer Flanders. To download this and other free printables, please visit https://flandersfamily.info.

Selected Bibliography

Resources for Children

Aesop. *The Grasshopper and the Ants*. Revised and edited by Jerry Pinkney. New York: Little Brown Books for Young Readers, 2015.

Bennett, William J., ed. "Work." *The Book of Virtues: A Treasury of Great Moral Stories*, 345–438. New York: Simon & Schuster, 1993.

Bunyan, John. *Pilgrim's Progress*. Edinburgh: Banner of Truth Trust, 1997.

Burton, Virginia Lee. *The Little House*. New York: Houghton Mifflin, 1981.

———. *Mike Mulligan and His Steam Shovel*. New York: Houghton Mifflin, 1967.

Cushman, Jean. *We Help Mommy*. New York: Golden Press, 1959.

Galdone, Paul. *The Little Red Hen*. New York: Clarion Books, 2001.

Howat, Irene. *Ten Boys Who Used Their Talents*. Fearn, Ross-shire, U.K.: Christian Focus, 2016.

———. *Ten Girls Who Made a Difference*. Fearn, Ross-shire, U.K.: Christian Focus, 2017.

Institute in Basic Youth Conflicts, Inc. *Character Sketches: From the Pages of Scripture Illustrated in the World of Nature, Vol. 1–3*. Chicago: Rand McNally, 1976.

Latham, Jean Lee. *Carry On, Mr. Bowditch*. New York: Houghton Mifflin, 1983.

Lobel, Arnold. *Frog and Toad Storybook Treasury*. New York: Harper & Row, 2013.

Maybury, Richard J. *Uncle Eric Talks About Personal Career and Financial Security*. Eagle, Ida.: Blue Stocking Press, 2004. Also see other "Uncle Eric" books.

Moody, Ralph. *Little Britches: Father and I Were Rangers*. Cynthiana, Ky.: Purple House Press, 2017. Also see other autobiographies by the same author.

Peet, Bill. *The Caboose Who Got Loose*. New York: Houghton Mifflin, 1999.

———. *Jennifer and Josephine*. New York: Houghton Mifflin, 1995.

Piper, Watty. *The Little Engine That Could*. Anniversary Edition. New York: Grosset & Dunlap, 2020.

Stein, Mini. *We Help Daddy*. New York: Golden Press, 1962.

Wilder, Laura Ingalls. *The Little House on the Prairie*. New York: Harper and Brothers, 1971. Also see other "Little House" books.

Resources for Parents

Barrett, Michael P. V. *The Next to Last Word*. Grand Rapids: Reformation Heritage Books, 2015.

Beckett, John D. *Mastering Monday: A Guide to Integrating Faith and Work*. Downers Grove, Ill.: InterVarsity Press, 2006.

Beeke, Joel R. *Parenting by God's Promises: How to Raise Children in the Covenant of Grace*. Orlando: Reformation Trust, 2011.

Beeke, Mary. *The Law of Kindness: Serving with Heart and Hands*. Grand Rapids: Reformation Heritage Books, 2007.

Bolt, John. *Economic Shalom: A Reformed Primer on Faith, Work, and Human Flourishing*. Grand Rapids: Christian's Library Press, 2013.

Brady, Gary. *Proverbs: Heavenly Wisdom*. Welwyn Garden City, U.K.: EP Books, 2003.

Burns, Jabez. *Mothers of the Wise and Good*. Vestavia Hills, Ala.: Solid Ground Christian Books, 2001.

Decker, Barbara. *Proverbs for Parenting*. Boise, Ida.: Lynn's Bookshelf, 1989.

Dobson, James. *The New Strong-Willed Child: Surviving Birth Through Adolescence*. Carol Stream, Ill.: Tyndale Momentum, 2004.

Doriani, Daniel. M. *Work: Its Purpose, Dignity, and Transformation*. Phillipsburg, N.J.: P&R, 2019.

Elliot, Elizabeth. "The Discipline of Work." *Joyful Surrender: 7 Disciplines for the Believer's Life*, 117–32. Grand Rapids: Revell, 2019.

Felton, Sandra. "Getting the Family to Cooperate." *The Messies Manual*, 118–26. Grand Rapids: Fleming H. Revell, 1984.

Hamilton Jr., James M. *Work and Our Labor in the Lord*. Wheaton, Ill.: Crossway, 2017.

Johnston, Robert K. *The Christian at Play*. Grand Rapids: Eerdmans, 1983.

Keller, Timothy. *Every Good Endeavor: Connecting Your Work to God's Work*. New York: Riverhead Books, 2012.

Koelman, Jacobus. *The Duties of Parents*. Grand Rapids: Baker Academic, 2003.

Larive, Armand. *After Sunday: A Theology of Work*. London: Continuum, 2004.

Leman, Kevin. *Have a New Kid by Friday*. Grand Rapids: Revell, 2018.

———. *Making Children Mind Without Losing Yours*. Grand Rapids: Revell, 2017.

Nichols, Stephen, ed. *Jonathan Edwards' Resolutions and Advice to Young Converts*. Phillipsburg, N.J.: P&R, 2001.

Pennings, Ray. *How Can I Serve God at Work?* Grand Rapids: Reformation Heritage Books, 2017.

Plowman, Ginger. *Heaven at Home*. Wapwallopen, Penn.: Shepherd Press, 2006.

Reinke, Tony. *Competing Spectacles: Treasuring Christ in the Media Age*. Wheaton, Ill.: Crossway, 2019.

Richardson, Alan. *The Biblical Doctrine of Work*. London: Living Church Books, 1963.

Ricker, Audrey, and Carolyn Crowder. *Whining: 3 Steps to Stopping It Before the Tears and Tantrums Start*. New York: Simon & Schuster, 2000.

Ryken, Leland. *Work and Leisure in Christian Perspective*. Portland, Ore.: Multnomah Press, 1987.

Schultz, Bob. *Created for Work: Practical Insights for Young Men*. Eugene, Ore.: Great Expectations Book Company, 2006.

Selvaggio, Anthony. *A Proverbs Driven Life: Timeless Wisdom for Your Words, Work, Wealth, and Relationships*. Wapwallopen, Penn.: Shepherd Press, 2008.

Tobias, Cynthia Ulrich. *You Can't Make Me [But I Can Be Persuaded]: Strategies for Bringing Out the Best in Your Strong-Willed Child.* Colorado Springs: Waterbrook Press, 2012.

Westcott, David. *Work Well: Live Well.* London: Marshall Pickering, 1996.

Wilkerson, Trisha. *Everyday Worship: Our Work, Heart and Jesus.* Fearn, Ross-shire, Scotland: Christian Focus, 2013.

Yates, Susan Alexander. *And Then I Had Kids.* Brentwood, Tenn.: Wolgemuth & Hyatt Publishers, 1988.